Loyalties
(Fifth Series Plays)

John Galsworthy

Contents

LOYALTIES
(FIFTH SERIES PLAYS)

BY

John Galsworthy

FIFTH SERIES PLAYS OF GALSWORTHY
LOYALTIES

By John Galsworthy

PERSONS OF THE PLAY

In the Order of Appearance

CHARLES WINSOR.................. Owner of Meldon Court, near Newmarket
LADY ADELA...................... His Wife
FERDINAND DE LEVIS.............. Young, rich, and new
TREISURE........................ Winsor's Butler
GENERAL CANYNGE................. A Racing Oracle
MARGARET ORME................... A Society Girl
CAPTAIN RONALD DANDY, D.S.O..... Retired
MABEL........................... His Wife
INSPECTOR DEDE.................. Of the County Constabulary
ROBERT.......................... Winsor's Footman
A CONSTABLE..................... Attendant on Dede
AUGUSTUS BOBBING................ A Clubman

LORD ST ERTH.................... A Peer of the Realm
A FOOTMAN...................... Of the Club
MAJOR COLFORD.................. A Brother Officer of Dancy's
EDWARD GRAVITER................ A Solicitor
A YOUNG CLERK.................. Of Twisden & Graviter's
GILMAN......................... A Large Grocer
JACOB TWISDEN.................. Senior Partner of Twisden & Graviter
RICARDOS....................... An Italian, in Wine

ACT I

SCENE I

The dressing-room of CHARLES WINSOR, owner of Meldon Court, near
Newmarket; about eleven-thirty at night. The room has pale grey
walls, unadorned; the curtains are drawn over a window Back Left
Centre. A bed lies along the wall, Left. An open door, Right Back,
leads into LADY ADELA's bedroom; a door, Right Forward, into a long
corridor, on to which abut rooms in a row, the whole length of the
house's left wing. WINSOR's dressing-table, with a light over it,
is Stage Right of the curtained window. Pyjamas are laid out on the
bed, which is turned back. Slippers are handy, and all the usual
gear of a well-appointed bed-dressing-room. CHARLES WINSOR, a tall,
fair, good-looking man about thirty-eight, is taking off a smoking
jacket.

WINSOR. Hallo! Adela!

V. OF LADY A. [From her bedroom] Hallo!

WINSOR. In bed?

V. OF LADY A. No.

> She appears in the doorway in under-garment and a wrapper. She,
> too, is fair, about thirty-five, rather delicious, and suggestive
> of porcelain.

WINSOR. Win at Bridge?

LADY A. No fear.

WINSOR. Who did?

LADY A. Lord St Erth and Ferdy De Levis.

WINSOR. That young man has too much luck--the young bounder won two
races to-day; and he's as rich as Croesus.

LADY A. Oh! Charlie, he did look so exactly as if he'd sold me a carpet
when I was paying him.

WINSOR. [Changing into slippers] His father did sell carpets,
wholesale, in the City.

LADY A. Really? And you say I haven't intuition! [With a finger on her
lips] Morison's in there.

WINSOR. [Motioning towards the door, which she shuts] Ronny Dancy took
a tenner off him, anyway, before dinner.

LADY A. No! How?

WINSOR. Standing jump on to a bookcase four feet high. De Levis had to pay up, and sneered at him for making money by parlour tricks. That young Jew gets himself disliked.

LADY A. Aren't you rather prejudiced?

WINSOR. Not a bit. I like Jews. That's not against him--rather the contrary these days. But he pushes himself. The General tells me he's deathly keen to get into the Jockey Club. [Taking off his tie] It's amusing to see him trying to get round old St Erth.

LADY A. If Lord St Erth and General Canynge backed him he'd get in if he did sell carpets!

WINSOR. He's got some pretty good horses. [Taking off his waistcoat] Ronny Dancy's on his bones again, I'm afraid. He had a bad day. When a chap takes to doing parlour stunts for a bet--it's a sure sign. What made him chuck the Army?

LADY A. He says it's too dull, now there's no fighting.

WINSOR. Well, he can't exist on backing losers.

LADY A. Isn't it just like him to get married now? He really is the most reckless person.

WINSOR. Yes. He's a queer chap. I've always liked him, but I've never quite made him out. What do you think of his wife?

LADY A. Nice child; awfully gone on him.

WINSOR. Is he?

LADY A. Quite indecently--both of them. [Nodding towards the wall, Left] They're next door.

WINSOR. Who's beyond them?

LADY A. De Levis; and Margaret Orme at the end. Charlie, do you realise that the bathroom out there has to wash those four?

WINSOR. I know.

LADY A. Your grandfather was crazy when he built this wing; six rooms in a row with balconies like an hotel, and only one bath--if we hadn't put ours in.

WINSOR. [Looking at his watch] Half-past eleven. [Yawns] Newmarket always makes me sleepy. You're keeping Morison up.

> LADY ADELA goes to the door, blowing a kiss. CHARLES goes up to his dressing-table and begins to brush his hair, sprinkling on essence. There is a knock on the corridor door.

Come in.

> DE LEVIS enters, clad in pyjamas and flowered dressing-gown. He is a dark, good-looking, rather Eastern young man. His face is long and disturbed.

Hallo! De Levis! Anything I can do for you?

DE LEVIS. [In a voice whose faint exoticism is broken by a vexed excitement] I say, I'm awfully sorry, Winsor, but I thought I'd better tell you at once. I've just had--er--rather a lot of money stolen.

WINSOR. What! [There is something of outrage in his tone and glance, as who should say: "In my house?"] How do you mean stolen?

DE LEVIS. I put it under my pillow and went to have a bath; when I came back it was gone.

WINSOR. Good Lord! How much?

DE LEVIS. Nearly a thousand-nine hundred and seventy, I think.

WINSOR. Phew! [Again the faint tone of outrage, that a man should have so much money about him].

DE LEVIS. I sold my Rosemary filly to-day on the course to Bentman the bookie, and he paid me in notes.

WINSOR. What? That weed Dancy gave you in the Spring?

DE LEVIS. Yes. But I tried her pretty high the other day; and she's in the Cambridgeshire. I was only out of my room a quarter of an hour, and I locked my door.

WINSOR. [Again outraged] You locked--

DE LEVIS. [Not seeing the fine shade] Yes, and had the key here. [He taps his pocket] Look here! [He holds out a pocket-book] It's been stuffed with my shaving papers.

WINSOR. [Between feeling that such things don't happen, and a sense that he will have to clear it up] This is damned awkward, De Levis.

DE LEVIS. [With steel in his voice] Yes. I should like it back.

WINSOR. Have you got the numbers of the notes?

DE LEVIS. No.

WINSOR. What were they?

DE LEVIS. One hundred, three fifties, and the rest tens and fives.

WINSOR. What d'you want me to do?

DE LEVIS. Unless there's anybody you think--

WINSOR. [Eyeing him] Is it likely?

DE Levis. Then I think the police ought to see my room. It's a lot of money.

WINSOR. Good Lord! We're not in Town; there'll be nobody nearer than Newmarket at this time of night--four miles.

    The door from the bedroom is suddenly opened and LADY ADELA appears.
    She has on a lace cap over her finished hair, and the wrapper.

LADY A. [Closing the door] What is it? Are you ill, Mr De Levis?

WINSOR. Worse; he's had a lot of money stolen. Nearly a thousand pounds.

LADY A. Gracious! Where?

DE LEVIS. From under my pillow, Lady Adela--my door was locked--I was in the bath-room.

LADY A. But how fearfully thrilling!

WINSOR. Thrilling! What's to be done? He wants it back.

LADY A. Of course! [With sudden realisation] Oh! But Oh! it's quite too unpleasant!

WINSOR. Yes! What am I to do? Fetch the servants out of their rooms? Search the grounds? It'll make the devil of a scandal.

DE LEVIS. Who's next to me?

LADY A. [Coldly] Oh! Mr De Levis!

WINSOR. Next to you? The Dancys on this side, and Miss Orme on the other. What's that to do with it?

DE LEVIS. They may have heard something.

WINSOR. Let's get them. But Dancy was down stairs when I came up. Get Morison, Adela! No. Look here! When was this exactly? Let's have as many alibis as we can.

DE LEVIS. Within the last twenty minutes, certainly.

WINSOR. How long has Morison been up with you?

LADY A. I came up at eleven, and rang for her at once.

WINSOR. [Looking at his watch] Half an hour. Then she's all right. Send her for Margaret and the Dancys--there's nobody else in this wing.

No; send her to bed. We don't want gossip. D'you mind going yourself, Adela?

LADY A. Consult General Canynge, Charlie.

WINSOR. Right. Could you get him too? D'you really want the police, De Levis?

DE LEVIS. [Stung by the faint contempt in his tone of voice] Yes, I do.

WINSOR. Then, look here, dear! Slip into my study and telephone to the police at Newmarket. There'll be somebody there; they're sure to have drunks. I'll have Treisure up, and speak to him. [He rings the bell].

    LADY ADELA goes out into her room and closes the door.

WINSOR. Look here, De Levis! This isn't an hotel. It's the sort of thing that doesn't happen in a decent house. Are you sure you're not mistaken, and didn't have them stolen on the course?

DE LEVIS. Absolutely. I counted them just before putting them under my pillow; then I locked the door and had the key here. There's only one door, you know.

WINSOR. How was your window?

DE LEVIS. Open.

WINSOR. [Drawing back the curtains of his own window] You've got a balcony like this. Any sign of a ladder or anything?

DE LEVIS. No.

WINSOR. It must have been done from the window, unless someone had a skeleton key. Who knew you'd got that money? Where did Kentman pay you?

DE LEVIS. Just round the corner in the further paddock.

WINSOR. Anybody about?

DE LEVIS. Oh, yes!

WINSOR. Suspicious?

DE LEVIS. I didn't notice anything.

WINSOR. You must have been marked down and followed here.

DE LEVIS. How would they know my room?

WINSOR. Might have got it somehow. [A knock from the corridor] Come in.

    TREISURE, the Butler, appears, a silent, grave man of almost supernatural conformity. DE LEVIS gives him a quick, hard look, noted and resented by WINSOR.

TREISURE. [To WINSOR] Yes, sir?

WINSOR. Who valets Mr De Levis?

TREISURE. Robert, Sir.

WINSOR. When was he up last?

TREISURE. In the ordinary course of things, about ten o'clock, sir.

WINSOR. When did he go to bed?

TREISURE. I dismissed at eleven.

WINSOR. But did he go?

TREISURE. To the best of my knowledge. Is there anything I can do, sir?

WINSOR. [Disregarding a sign from DE LEVIS] Look here, Treisure, Mr De Levis has had a large sum of money taken from his bedroom within the last half hour.

TREISURE. Indeed, Sir!

WINSOR. Robert's quite all right, isn't he?

TREISURE. He is, sir.

DE LEVIS. How do you know?

    TREISURE's eyes rest on DE LEVIS.

TREISURE. I am a pretty good judge of character, sir, if you'll excuse me.

WINSOR. Look here, De Levis, eighty or ninety notes must have been pretty bulky. You didn't have them on you at dinner?

DE LEVIS. No.

WINSOR. Where did you put them?

DE LEVIS. In a boot, and the boot in my suitcase, and locked it.

TREISURE smiles faintly.

WINSOR. [Again slightly outraged by such precautions in his house] And you found it locked--and took them from there to put under your pillow?

DE LEVIS. Yes.

WINSOR. Run your mind over things, Treisure--has any stranger been about?

TREISURE. No, Sir.

WINSOR. This seems to have happened between 11.15 and 11.30. Is that right? [DE LEVIS nods] Any noise-anything outside-anything suspicious anywhere?

TREISURE. [Running his mind--very still] No, sir.

WINSOR. What time did you shut up?

TREISURE. I should say about eleven-fifteen, sir. As soon as Major Colford and Captain Dancy had finished billiards. What was Mr De Levis doing out of his room, if I may ask, sir?

WINSOR. Having a bath; with his room locked and the key in his pocket.

TREISURE. Thank you, sir.

DE LEVIS. [Conscious of indefinable suspicion] Damn it! What do you mean? I WAS!

TREISURE. I beg your pardon, sir.

WINSOR. [Concealing a smile] Look here, Treasure, it's infernally awkward for everybody.

TREISURE. It is, sir.

WINSOR. What do you suggest?

TREISURE. The proper thing, sir, I suppose, would be a cordon and a complete search--in our interests.

WINSOR. I entirely refuse to suspect anybody.

TREISURE. But if Mr De Levis feels otherwise, sir?

DE LEVIS. [Stammering] I? All I know is--the money was there, and it's gone.

WINSOR. [Compunctious] Quite! It's pretty sickening for you. But so it is for anybody else. However, we must do our best to get it back for you.

> A knock on the door.

WINSOR. Hallo!

> TREISURE opens the door, and GENERAL. CANYNGE enters.

Oh! It's you, General. Come in. Adela's told you?

> GENERAL CANYNGE nods. He is a slim man of about sixty, very well preserved, intensely neat and self-contained, and still in evening dress. His eyelids droop slightly, but his eyes are keen and his

expression astute.

WINSOR. Well, General, what's the first move?

CANYNGE. [Lifting his eyebrows] Mr De Levis presses the matter?

DE Levis. [Flicked again] Unless you think it's too plebeian of me,
General Canynge--a thousand pounds.

CANYNGE. [Drily] Just so! Then we must wait for the police, WINSOR.
Lady Adela has got through to them. What height are these rooms from the
ground, Treisure?

TREISURE. Twenty-three feet from the terrace, sir.

CANYNGE. Any ladders near?

TREISURE. One in the stables, Sir, very heavy. No others within three
hundred yards.

CANYNGE. Just slip down, and see whether that's been moved.

TREISURE. Very good, General. [He goes out.]

DE LEVIS. [Uneasily] Of course, he--I suppose you--

WINSOR. We do.

CANYNGE. You had better leave this in our hands, De Levis.

DE LEVIS. Certainly; only, the way he--

WINSOR. [Curtly] Treisure has been here since he was a boy. I should as soon suspect myself.

DE LEVIS. [Looking from one to the other--with sudden anger] You seem to think--! What was I to do? Take it lying down and let whoever it is get clear off? I suppose it's natural to want my money back?

CANYNGE looks at his nails; WINSOR out of the window.

WINSOR. [Turning] Of course, De Levis!

DE LEVIS. [Sullenly] Well, I'll go to my room. When the police come, perhaps you'll let me know. He goes out.

WINSOR. Phew! Did you ever see such a dressing-gown?

The door is opened. LADY ADELA and MARGARET ORME come in. The
latter is a vivid young lady of about twenty-five in a vivid
wrapper; she is smoking a cigarette.

LADY A. I've told the Dancys--she was in bed. And I got through to Newmarket, Charles, and Inspector Dede is coming like the wind on a motor cycle.

MARGARET. Did he say "like the wind," Adela? He must have imagination. Isn't this gorgeous? Poor little Ferdy!

WINSOR. [Vexed] You might take it seriously, Margaret; it's pretty beastly for us all. What time did you come up?

MARGARET. I came up with Adela. Am I suspected, Charles? How thrilling!

WINSOR. Did you hear anything?

MARGARET. Only little Ferdy splashing.

WINSOR. And saw nothing?

MARGARET. Not even that, alas!

LADY A. [With a finger held up] Leste! Un peu leste! Oh! Here are the Dancys. Come in, you two!

> MABEL and RONALD DANCY enter. She is a pretty young woman with bobbed hair, fortunately, for she has just got out of bed, and is in her nightgown and a wrapper. DANCY is in his smoking jacket. He has a pale, determined face with high cheekbones, small, deep-set dark eyes, reddish crisp hair, and looks like a horseman.

WINSOR. Awfully sorry to disturb you, Mrs Dancy; but I suppose you and Ronny haven't heard anything. De Levis's room is just beyond Ronny's dressing-room, you know.

MABEL. I've been asleep nearly half an hour, and Ronny's only just come up.

CANYNGE. Did you happen to look out of your window, Mrs Dancy?

MABEL. Yes. I stood there quite five minutes.

CANYNGE. When?

MABEL. Just about eleven, I should think. It was raining hard then.

CANYNGE. Yes, it's just stopped. You saw nothing?

MABEL. No.

DANCY. What time does he say the money was taken?

WINSOR. Between the quarter and half past. He'd locked his door and had the key with him.

MARGARET. How quaint! Just like an hotel. Does he put his boots out?

LADY A. Don't be so naughty, Meg.

CANYNGE. When exactly did you come up, Dance?

DANCY. About ten minutes ago. I'd only just got into my dressing-room before Lady Adela came. I've been writing letters in the hall since Colford and I finished billiards.

CANYNGE. You weren't up for anything in between?

DANCY. No.

MARGARET. The mystery of the grey room.

DANCY. Oughtn't the grounds to be searched for footmarks?

CANYNGE. That's for the police.

DANCY. The deuce! Are they coming?

CANYNGE. Directly. [A knock] Yes?

    TREISURE enters.

Well?

TREISURE. The ladder has not been moved, General. There isn't a sign.

WINSOR. All right. Get Robert up, but don't say anything to him. By the way, we're expecting the police.

TREISURE. I trust they will not find a mare's nest, sir, if I may say so.

　　He goes.

WINSOR. De Levis has got wrong with Treisure. [Suddenly] But, I say, what would any of us have done if we'd been in his shoes?

MARGARET. A thousand pounds? I can't even conceive having it.

DANCY. We probably shouldn't have found it out.

LADY A. No--but if we had.

DANCY. Come to you--as he did.

WINSOR. Yes; but there's a way of doing things.

CANYNGE. We shouldn't have wanted the police.

MARGARET. No. That's it. The hotel touch.

LADY A. Poor young man; I think we're rather hard on him.

WINSOR. He sold that weed you gave him, Dancy, to Kentman, the bookie, and these were the proceeds.

DANCY. Oh!

WINSOR. He'd tried her high, he said.

DANCY. [Grimly] He would.

MABEL. Oh! Ronny, what bad luck!

WINSOR. He must have been followed here. [At the window] After rain like that, there ought to be footmarks.

    The splutter of a motor cycle is heard.

MARGARET. Here's the wind!

WINSOR. What's the move now, General?

CANYNGE. You and I had better see the Inspector in De Levis's room, WINSOR. [To the others] If you'll all be handy, in case he wants to put questions for himself.

MARGARET. I hope he'll want me; it's just too thrilling.

DANCY. I hope he won't want me; I'm dog-tired. Come on, Mabel. [He puts his arm in his wife's].

CANYNGE. Just a minute, Charles.

    He draws dose to WINSOR as the others are departing to their rooms.

WINSOR. Yes, General?

CANYNGE. We must be careful with this Inspector fellow. If he pitches hastily on somebody in the house it'll be very disagreeable.

WINSOR. By Jove! It will.

CANYNGE. We don't want to rouse any ridiculous suspicion.

WINSOR. Quite. [A knock] Come in!

TREISURE enters.

TREISURE. Inspector Dede, Sir.

WINSOR. Show him in.

TREISURE. Robert is in readiness, sir; but I could swear he knows nothing about it.

WINSOR. All right.

TREISURE re-opens the door, and says "Come in, please." The INSPECTOR enters, blue, formal, moustachioed, with a peaked cap in his hand.

WINSOR. Good evening, Inspector. Sorry to have brought you out at this time of night.

INSPECTOR. Good evenin', sir. Mr WINSOR? You're the owner here, I think?

WINSOR. Yes. General Canynge.

INSPECTOR. Good evenin', General. I understand, a large sum of money?

WINSOR. Yes. Shall we go straight to the room it was taken from? One of my guests, Mr De Levis. It's the third room on the left.

CANYNGE. We've not been in there yet, Inspector; in fact, we've done nothing, except to find out that the stable ladder has not been moved. We haven't even searched the grounds.

INSPECTOR. Right, sir; I've brought a man with me.

They go out.

CURTAIN. And interval of a Minute.

SCENE II

[The same set is used for this Scene, with the different arrangement of furniture, as specified.]

The bedroom of DE LEVIS is the same in shape as WINSOR'S dressing-room, except that there is only one door--to the corridor. The furniture, however, is differently arranged; a small four-poster bedstead stands against the wall, Right Back, jutting into the room. A chair, on which DE LEVIS's clothes are thrown, stands at its foot. There is a dressing-table against the wall to the left of the open windows, where the curtains are drawn back and a stone balcony is seen. Against the wall to the right of the window is a chest of drawers, and a washstand is against the wall, Left. On a small table to the right of the bed

an electric reading lamp is turned up, and there is a light over
the dressing-table. The INSPECTOR is standing plumb centre
looking at the bed, and DE LEVIS by the back of the chair at the
foot of the bed. WINSOR and CANYNGE are close to the door, Right
Forward.

INSPECTOR. [Finishing a note] Now, sir, if this is the room as you left
it for your bath, just show us exactly what you did after takin' the
pocket-book from the suit case. Where was that, by the way?

DE LEVIS. [Pointing] Where it is now--under the dressing-table.

He comes forward to the front of the chair, opens the pocket-book,
goes through the pretence of counting his shaving papers, closes the
pocket-book, takes it to the head of the bed and slips it under the
pillow. Makes the motion of taking up his pyjamas, crosses below
the INSPECTOR to the washstand, takes up a bath sponge, crosses to
the door, takes out the key, opens the door.

INSPECTOR. [Writing]. We now have the room as it was when the theft was
committed. Reconstruct accordin' to 'uman nature, gentlemen--assumin'
the thief to be in the room, what would he try first?--the clothes, the
dressin'-table, the suit case, the chest of drawers, and last the bed.

He moves accordingly, examining the glass on the dressing-table, the
surface of the suit cases, and the handles of the drawers, with a
spy-glass, for finger-marks.

CANYNGE. [Sotto voce to WINSOR] The order would have been just the
other way.

The INSPECTOR goes on hands and knees and examines the carpet
between the window and the bed.

DE LEVIS. Can I come in again?

INSPECTOR. [Standing up] Did you open the window, sir, or was it open when you first came in?

DE LEVIS. I opened it.

INSPECTOR. Drawin' the curtains back first?

DE LEVIS. Yes.

INSPECTOR. [Sharply] Are you sure there was nobody in the room already?

DE LEVIS. [Taken aback] I don't know. I never thought. I didn't look under the bed, if you mean that.

INSPECTOR. [Jotting] Did not look under bed. Did you look under it after the theft?

DE LEVIS. No. I didn't.

INSPECTOR. Ah! Now, what did you do after you came back from your bath? Just give us that precisely.

DE LEVIS. Locked the door and left the key in. Put back my sponge, and took off my dressing-gown and put it there. [He points to the footrails of the bed] Then I drew the curtains, again.

INSPECTOR. Shutting the window?

DE LEVIS. No. I got into bed, felt for my watch to see the time. My hand struck the pocket-book, and somehow it felt thinner. I took it out, looked into it, and found the notes gone, and these shaving papers instead.

INSPECTOR. Let me have a look at those, sir. [He applies the spy-glasses] And then?

DE LEVIS. I think I just sat on the bed.

INSPECTOR. Thinkin' and cursin' a bit, I suppose. Ye-es?

DE LEVIS. Then I put on my dressing-gown and went straight to Mr WIN-SOR.

INSPECTOR. Not lockin' the door?

DE LEVIS. No.

INSPECTOR. Exactly. [With a certain finality] Now, sir, what time did you come up?

DE LEVIS. About eleven.

INSPECTOR. Precise, if you can give it me.

DE LEVIS. Well, I know it was eleven-fifteen when I put my watch under my pillow, before I went to the bath, and I suppose I'd been about a quarter of an hour undressing. I should say after eleven, if anything.

INSPECTOR. Just undressin'? Didn't look over your bettin' book?

DE LEVIS. No.

INSPECTOR. No prayers or anything?

DE LEVIS. No.

INSPECTOR. Pretty slippy with your undressin' as a rule?

DE LEVIS. Yes. Say five past eleven.

INSPECTOR. Mr WINSOR, what time did the gentleman come to you?

WINSOR. Half-past eleven.

INSPECTOR. How do you fix that, sir?

WINSOR. I'd just looked at the time, and told my wife to send her maid off.

INSPECTOR. Then we've got it fixed between 11.15 and 11.30. [Jots] Now, sir, before we go further I'd like to see your butler and the footman that valets this gentleman.

WINSOR. [With distaste] Very well, Inspector; only--my butler has been with us from a boy.

INSPECTOR. Quite so. This is just clearing the ground, sir.

WINSOR. General, d'you mind touching that bell?

CANYNGE rings a bell by the bed.

INSPECTOR. Well, gentlemen, there are four possibilities. Either the thief was here all the time, waiting under the bed, and slipped out after this gentleman had gone to Mr WINSOR. Or he came in with a key that fits the lock; and I'll want to see all the keys in the house. Or he came in with a skeleton key and out by the window, probably droppin' from the balcony. Or he came in by the window with a rope or ladder and out the same way. [Pointing] There's a footmark here from a big boot which has been out of doors since it rained.

CANYNGE. Inspector--you er--walked up to the window when you first came into the room.

INSPECTOR. [Stiffly] I had not overlooked that, General.

CANYNGE. Of course.

A knock on the door relieves a certain tension,

WINSOR. Come in.

The footman ROBERT, a fresh-faced young man, enters, followed by TREISURE.

INSPECTOR. You valet Mr--Mr De Levis, I think?

ROBERT. Yes, sir.

INSPECTOR. At what time did you take his clothes and boots?

ROBERT. Ten o'clock, sir.

INSPECTOR. [With a pounce] Did you happen to look under his bed?

ROBERT. No, sir.

INSPECTOR. Did you come up again, to bring the clothes back?

ROBERT. No, sir; they're still downstairs.

INSPECTOR. Did you come up again for anything?

ROBERT. No, Sir.

INSPECTOR. What time did you go to bed?

ROBERT. Just after eleven, Sir.

INSPECTOR. [Scrutinising him] Now, be careful. Did you go to bed at all?

ROBERT. No, Sir.

INSPECTOR. Then why did you say you did? There's been a theft here, and anything you say may be used against you.

ROBERT. Yes, Sir. I meant, I went to my room.

INSPECTOR. Where is your room?

ROBERT. On the ground floor, at the other end of the right wing, sir.

WINSOR. It's the extreme end of the house from this, Inspector. He's with the other two footmen.

INSPECTOR. Were you there alone?

ROBERT. No, Sir. Thomas and Frederick was there too.

TREISURE. That's right; I've seen them.

INSPECTOR. [Holding up his hand for silence] Were you out of the room again after you went in?

ROBERT. No, Sir.

INSPECTOR. What were you doing, if you didn't go to bed?

ROBERT. [To WINSOR] Beggin' your pardon, Sir, we were playin' Bridge.

INSPECTOR. Very good. You can go. I'll see them later on.

ROBERT. Yes, Sir. They'll say the same as me. He goes out, leaving a smile on the face of all except the INSPECTOR and DE LEVIS.

INSPECTOR. [Sharply] Call him back.

   TREISURE calls "Robert," and the FOOTMAN re-enters.

ROBERT. Yes, Sir?

INSPECTOR. Did you notice anything particular about Mr De Levis's clothes?

ROBERT. Only that they were very good, Sir.

INSPECTOR. I mean--anything peculiar?

ROBERT. [After reflection] Yes, Sir.

INSPECTOR. Well?

ROBERT. A pair of his boots this evenin' was reduced to one, sir.

INSPECTOR. What did you make of that?

ROBERT. I thought he might have thrown the other at a cat or something.

INSPECTOR. Did you look for it?

ROBERT. No, Sir; I meant to draw his attention to it in the morning.

INSPECTOR. Very good.

ROBERT. Yes, Sir. [He goes again.]

INSPECTOR. [Looking at DE LEVIS] Well, sir, there's your story corroborated.

DE LEVIS. [Stiffly] I don't know why it should need corroboration, Inspector.

INSPECTOR. In my experience, you can never have too much of that. [To WINSOR] I understand there's a lady in the room on this side [pointing Left] and a gentleman on this [pointing Right] Were they in their rooms?

WINSOR. Miss Orme was; Captain Dancy not.

INSPECTOR. Do they know of the affair?

WINSOR. Yes.

INSPECTOR. Well, I'd just like the keys of their doors for a minute. My man will get them.

He goes to the door, opens it, and speaks to a constable in the corridor.

[To TREISURE] You can go with him.

TREISURE goes Out.

In the meantime I'll just examine the balcony.

He goes out on the balcony, followed by DE LEVIS.

WINSOR. [To CANYNGE] Damn De Levis and his money! It's deuced invidious, all this, General.

CANYNGE. The Inspector's no earthly.

There is a simultaneous re-entry of the INSPECTOR from the balcony and of TREISURE and the CONSTABLE from the corridor.

CONSTABLE. [Handing key] Room on the left, Sir. [Handing key] Room on the right, sir.

The INSPECTOR tries the keys in the door, watched with tension by the others. The keys fail.

INSPECTOR. Put them back.

Hands keys to CONSTABLE, who goes out, followed by TREISURE.

I'll have to try every key in the house, sir.

WINSOR. Inspector, do you really think it necessary to disturb the whole house and knock up all my guests? It's most disagreeable, all this, you know. The loss of the money is not such a great matter. Mr De Levis has a very large income.

CANYNGE. You could get the numbers of the notes from Kentman the bookmaker, Inspector; he'll probably have the big ones, anyway.

INSPECTOR. [Shaking his head] A bookie. I don't suppose he will, sir. It's come and go with them, all the time.

WINSOR. We don't want a Meldon Court scandal, Inspector.

INSPECTOR. Well, Mr WINSOR, I've formed my theory.

As he speaks, DE LEVIS comes in from the balcony.

And I don't say to try the keys is necessary to it; but strictly, I ought to exhaust the possibilities.

WINSOR. What do you say, De Levis? D'you want everybody in the house knocked up so that their keys can be tried?

DE LEVIS. [Whose face, since his return, expresses a curious excitement] No, I don't.

INSPECTOR. Very well, gentlemen. In my opinion the thief walked in before the door was locked, probably during dinner; and was under the bed. He escaped by dropping from the balcony--the creeper at that corner [he points stage Left] has been violently wrenched. I'll go down now, and examine the grounds, and I'll see you again Sir. [He makes another entry in his note-book] Goodnight, then, gentlemen!

CANYNGE. Good-night!

WINSOR. [With relief] I'll come with you, Inspector.

He escorts him to the door, and they go out.

DE LEVIS. [Suddenly] General, I know who took them.

CANYNGE. The deuce you do! Are you following the Inspector's theory?

DE LEVIS. [Contemptuously] That ass! [Pulling the shaving papers out of the case] No! The man who put those there was clever and cool enough to wrench that creeper off the balcony, as a blind. Come and look here, General. [He goes to the window; the GENERAL follows. DE LEVIS points stage Right] See the rail of my balcony, and the rail of the next? [He holds up the cord of his dressing-gown, stretching his arms out] I've measured it with this. Just over seven feet, that's all! If a man can take a standing jump on to a narrow bookcase four feet high and balance there, he'd make nothing of that. And, look here! [He goes out on the balcony and returns with a bit of broken creeper in his hand, and holds it out into the light] Someone's stood on that--the stalk's crushed--the inner corner too, where he'd naturally stand when he took his jump back.

CANYNGE. [After examining it--stiffly] That other balcony is young Dancy's, Mr De Levis; a soldier and a gentleman. This is an extraordinary insinuation.

DE LEVIS. Accusation.

CANYNGE. What!

DE LEVIS. I have intuitions, General; it's in my blood. I see the whole thing. Dancy came up, watched me into the bathroom, tried my door, slipped back into his dressing-room, saw my window was open, took that jump, sneaked the notes, filled the case up with these, wrenched the creeper there [He points stage Left] for a blind, jumped back, and slipped downstairs again. It didn't take him four minutes altogether.

CANYNGE. [Very gravely] This is outrageous, De Levis. Dancy says he was downstairs all the time. You must either withdraw unreservedly, or I must confront you with him.

DE LEVIS. If he'll return the notes and apologise, I'll do nothing-- except cut him in future. He gave me that filly, you know, as a hopeless weed, and he's been pretty sick ever since, that he was such a flat as not to see how good she was. Besides, he's hard up, I know.

CANYNGE. [After a vexed turn up and down the room] It's mad, sir, to jump to conclusions like this.

DE LEVIS. Not so mad as the conclusion Dancy jumped to when he lighted on my balcony.

CANYNGE. Nobody could have taken this money who did not know you had it.

DE LEVIS. How do you know that he didn't?

CANYNGE. Do you know that he did?

DE LEVIS. I haven't the least doubt of it.

CANYNGE. Without any proof. This is very ugly, De Levis. I must tell WINSOR.

DE LEVIS. [Angrily] Tell the whole blooming lot. You think I've no feelers, but I've felt the atmosphere here, I can tell you, General. If I were in Dancy's shoes and he in mine, your tone to me would be very different.

CANYNGE. [Suavely frigid] I'm not aware of using any tone, as you call it. But this is a private house, Mr De Levis, and something is due to our host and to the esprit de corps that exists among gentlemen.

DE LEVIS. Since when is a thief a gentleman? Thick as thieves--a good motto, isn't it?

CANYNGE. That's enough! [He goes to the door, but stops before opening it] Now, look here! I have some knowledge of the world. Once an accusation like this passes beyond these walls no one can foresee the consequences. Captain Dancy is a gallant fellow, with a fine record as a soldier; and only just married. If he's as innocent as--Christ--mud will stick to him, unless the real thief is found. In the old days of swords, either you or he would not have gone out of this room alive. It you persist in this absurd accusation, you will both of you go out of this room dead in the eyes of Society: you for bringing it, he for being the object of it.

DE LEVIS. Society! Do you think I don't know that I'm only tolerated for my money? Society can't add injury to insult and have my money as well, that's all. If the notes are restored I'll keep my mouth shut; if they're not, I shan't. I'm certain I'm right. I ask nothing better than to be confronted with Dancy; but, if you prefer it, deal with him in your own way--for the sake of your esprit de corps.

CANYNGE. 'Pon my soul, Mr De Levis, you go too far.

DE LEVIS. Not so far as I shall go, General Canynge, if those notes aren't given back.

WINSOR comes in.

WINSOR. Well, De Levis, I'm afraid that's all we can do for the present.

So very sorry this should have happened in my house.

CANYNGE. [Alter a silence] There's a development, WINSOR. Mr De Levis accuses one of your guests.

WINSOR. What?

CANYNGE. Of jumping from his balcony to this, taking the notes, and jumping back. I've done my best to dissuade him from indulging the fancy--without success. Dancy must be told.

DE LEVIS. You can deal with Dancy in your own way. All I want is the money back.

CANYNGE. [Drily] Mr De Levis feels that he is only valued for his money, so that it is essential for him to have it back.

WINSOR. Damn it! This is monstrous, De Levis. I've known Ronald Dancy since he was a boy.

CANYNGE. You talk about adding injury to insult, De Levis. What do you call such treatment of a man who gave you the mare out of which you made this thousand pounds?

DE LEVIS. I didn't want the mare; I took her as a favour.

CANYNGE. With an eye to possibilities, I venture to think--the principle guides a good many transactions.

DE LEVIS. [As if flicked on a raw spot] In my race, do you mean?

CANYNGE. [Coldly] I said nothing of the sort.

DE LEVIS. No; you don't say these things, any of you.

CANYNGE. Nor did I think it.

DE LEVIS. Dancy does.

WINSOR. Really, De Levis, if this is the way you repay hospitality--

DE LEVIS. Hospitality that skins my feelings and costs me a thousand pounds!

CANYNGE. Go and get Dancy, WINSOR; but don't say anything to him.

WINSOR goes out.

CANYNGE. Perhaps you will kindly control yourself, and leave this to me.

DE LEVIS turns to the window and lights a cigarette. WINSOR comes back, followed by DANCY.

CANYNGE. For WINSOR's sake, Dancy, we don't want any scandal or fuss about this affair. We've tried to make the police understand that. To my mind the whole thing turns on our finding who knew that De Levis had this money. It's about that we want to consult you.

WINSOR. Kentman paid De Levis round the corner in the further paddock, he says.

DE LEVIS turns round from the window, so that he and DANCY are staring at each other.

CANYNGE. Did you hear anything that throws light, Dancy? As it was your filly originally, we thought perhaps you might.

DANCY. I? No.

CANYNGE. Didn't hear of the sale on the course at all?

DANCY. No.

CANYNGE. Then you can't suggest any one who could have known? Nothing else was taken, you see.

DANCY. De Levis is known to be rolling, as I am known to be stony.

CANYNGE. There are a good many people still rolling, besides Mr De Levis, but not many people with so large a sum in their pocket-books.

DANCY. He won two races.

DE LEVIS. Do you suggest that I bet in ready money?

DANCY. I don't know how you bet, and I don't care.

CANYNGE. You can't help us, then?

DANCY. No. I can't. Anything else? [He looks fixedly at DE LEVIS].

CANYNGE. [Putting his hand on DANCY's arm] Nothing else, thank you, Dancy.

> DANCY goes. CANYNGE puts his hand up to his face. A moment's silence.

WINSOR. You see, De Levis? He didn't even know you'd got the money.

DE LEVIS. Very conclusive.

WINSOR. Well! You are--!

There is a knock on the door, and the INSPECTOR enters.

INSPECTOR. I'm just going, gentlemen. The grounds, I'm sorry to say, have yielded nothing. It's a bit of a puzzle.

CANYNGE. You've searched thoroughly?

INSPECTOR. We have, General. I can pick up nothing near the terrace.

WINSOR. [After a look at DE LEVIS, whose face expresses too much] H'm! You'll take it up from the other end, then, Inspector?

INSPECTOR. Well, we'll see what we can do with the bookmakers about the numbers, sir. Before I go, gentlemen--you've had time to think it over-- there's no one you suspect in the house, I suppose?

DE LEVIS's face is alive and uncertain. CANYNGE is staring at him very fixedly.

WINSOR. [Emphatically] No.

DE LEVIS turns and goes out on to the balcony.

INSPECTOR. If you're coming in to the racing to-morrow, sir, you might give us a call. I'll have seen Kentman by then.

WINSOR. Right you are, Inspector. Good night, and many thanks.

INSPECTOR. You're welcome, sir. [He goes out.]

WINSOR. Gosh! I thought that chap [With a nod towards the balcony] was going to--! Look here, General, we must stop his tongue. Imagine it going the rounds. They may never find the real thief, you know. It's the very devil for Dancy.

CANYNGE. WINSOR! Dancy's sleeve was damp.

WINSOR. How d'you mean?

CANYNGE. Quite damp. It's been raining.

The two look at each other.

WINSOR. I--I don't follow-- [His voice is hesitative and lower, showing that he does].

CANYNGE. It was coming down hard; a minute out in it would have been enough--[He motions with his chin towards the balcony].

WINSOR. [Hastily] He must have been out on his balcony since.

CANYNGE. It stopped before I came up, half an hour ago.

WINSOR. He's been leaning on the wet stone, then.

CANYNGE. With the outside of the upper part of the arm?

WINSOR. Against the wall, perhaps. There may be a dozen explanations. [Very low and with great concentration] I entirely and absolutely refuse to believe anything of the sort against Ronald Dancy in my house. Dash it, General, we must do as we'd be done by. It hits us all--it hits us all. The thing's intolerable.

CANYNGE. I agree. Intolerable. [Raising his voice] Mr De Levis!

DE LEVIS returns into view, in the centre of the open window.

CANYNGE. [With cold decision] Young Dancy was an officer and is a gentleman; this insinuation is pure supposition, and you must not make it. Do you understand me?

DE LEVIS. My tongue is still mine, General, if my money isn't!

CANYNGE. [Unmoved] Must not. You're a member of three Clubs, you want to be member of a fourth. No one who makes such an insinuation against a fellow-guest in a country house, except on absolute proof, can do so without complete ostracism. Have we your word to say nothing?

DE LEVIS. Social blackmail? H'm!

CANYNGE. Not at all--simple warning. If you consider it necessary in your interests to start this scandal-no matter how, we shall consider it necessary in ours to dissociate ourselves completely from one who so recklessly disregards the unwritten code.

DE LEVIS. Do you think your code applies to me? Do you, General?

CANYNGE. To anyone who aspires to be a gentleman, Sir.

DE LEVIS. Ah! But you haven't known me since I was a boy.

CANYNGE. Make up your mind.

A pause.

DE LEVIS. I'm not a fool, General. I know perfectly well that you can get me outed.

CANYNGE. [Icily] Well?

DE LEVIS. [Sullenly] I'll say nothing about it, unless I get more proof.

CANYNGE. Good! We have implicit faith in Dancy.

There is a moment's encounter of eyes; the GENERAL'S steady, shrewd, impassive; WINSOR'S angry and defiant; DE LEVIS's mocking, a little triumphant, malicious. Then CANYNGE and WINSOR go to the door, and pass out.

DE LEVIS. [To himself] Rats!

CURTAIN

ACT II

SCENE I

Afternoon, three weeks later, in the card room of a London Club. A fire is burning, Left. A door, Right, leads to the billiard-room. Rather Left of Centre, at a card table, LORD ST ERTH, an old John Bull, sits facing the audience; to his right is GENERAL CANYNGE, to his left AUGUSTUS BORRING, an essential Clubman, about thirty-five years old, with a very slight and rather becoming stammer or click in his speech. The fourth Bridge player, CHARLES WINSOR, stands with his back to the fire.

BORRING. And the r-rub.

WINSOR. By George! You do hold cards, Borring.

ST ERTH. [Who has lost] Not a patch on the old whist--this game. Don't know why I play it--never did.

CANYNGE. St Erth, shall we raise the flag for whist again?

WINSOR. No go, General. You can't go back on pace. No getting a man to walk when he knows he can fly. The young men won't look at it.

BORRING. Better develop it so that t-two can sit out, General.

ST ERTH. We ought to have stuck to the old game. Wish I'd gone to Newmarket, Canynge, in spite of the weather.

CANYNGE. [Looking at his watch] Let's hear what's won the Cambridgeshire. Ring, won't you, WINSOR? [WINSOR rings.]

ST ERTH. By the way, Canynge, young De Levis was blackballed.

CANYNGE. What!

ST ERTH. I looked in on my way down.

CANYNGE sits very still, and WINSOR utters a disturbed sound.

BORRING. But of c-course he was, General. What did you expect?

A FOOTMAN enters.

FOOTMAN. Yes, my lord?

ST ERTH. What won the Cambridgeshire?

FOOTMAN. Rosemary, my lord. Sherbet second; Barbizon third. Nine to one the winner.

WINSOR. Thank you. That's all.

FOOTMAN goes.

BORRING. Rosemary! And De Levis sold her! But he got a good p-price, I suppose.

The other three look at him.

ST ERTH. Many a slip between price and pocket, young man.

CANYNGE. Cut! [They cut].

BORRING. I say, is that the yarn that's going round about his having had a lot of m-money stolen in a country house? By Jove! He'll be pretty s-sick.

WINSOR. You and I, Borring.

He sits down in CANYNGE'S chair, and the GENERAL takes his place by the fire.

BORRING. Phew! Won't Dancy be mad! He gave that filly away to save her keep. He was rather pleased to find somebody who'd take her. Bentman must have won a p-pot. She was at thirty-threes a fortnight ago.

ST ERTH. All the money goes to fellows who don't know a horse from a haystack.

CANYNGE. [Profoundly] And care less. Yes! We want men racing to whom a horse means something.

BORRING. I thought the horse m-meant the same to everyone, General--chance to get the b-better of one's neighbour.

CANYNGE. [With feeling] The horse is a noble animal, sir, as you'd know if you'd owed your life to them as often as I have.

BORRING. They always try to take mine, General. I shall never belong to the noble f-fellowship of the horse.

ST ERTH. [Drily] Evidently. Deal!

As BORRING begins to deal the door is opened and MAJOR COLFORD appears--a lean and moustached cavalryman.

BORRING. Hallo, C-Colford.

COLFORD. General!

Something in the tone of his voice brings them all to a standstill.

COLFORD. I want your advice. Young De Levis in there [He points to the billiard-room from which he has just come] has started a blasphemous story--

CANYNGE. One moment. Mr Borring, d'you mind--

COLFORD. It makes no odds, General. Four of us in there heard him.
He's saying it was Ronald Dancy robbed him down at WINSOR's. The
fellow's mad over losing the price of that filly now she's won the
Cambridgeshire.

BORRING. [All ears] Dancy! Great S-Scott!

COLFORD. Dancy's in the Club. If he hadn't been I'd have taken it on
myself to wring the bounder's neck.

> WINSOR and BORRING have risen. ST ERTH alone remains seated.

CANYNGE. [After consulting ST ERTH with a look] Ask De Levis to be good
enough to come in here. Borring, you might see that Dancy doesn't leave
the Club. We shall want him. Don't say anything to him, and use your
tact to keep people off.

> BORRING goes out, followed by COLFORD. WINSOR. Result of hearing
> he was black-balled--pretty slippy.

CANYNGE. St Erth, I told you there was good reason when I asked you to
back young De Levis. WINSOR and I knew of this insinuation; I wanted to
keep his tongue quiet. It's just wild assertion; to have it bandied
about was unfair to Dancy. The duel used to keep people's tongues in
order.

ST ERTH. H'm! It never settled anything, except who could shoot
straightest.

COLFORD. [Re-appearing] De Levis says he's nothing to add to what he
said to you before, on the subject.

CANYNGE. Kindly tell him that if he wishes to remain a member of this Club he must account to the Committee for such a charge against a fellow-member. Four of us are here, and form a quorum.

　　　COLFORD goes out again.

ST ERTH. Did Kentman ever give the police the numbers of those notes, WINSOR?

WINSOR. He only had the numbers of two--the hundred, and one of the fifties.

ST ERTH. And they haven't traced 'em?

WINSOR. Not yet.

　　　As he speaks, DE LEVIS comes in. He is in a highly-coloured, not to
　　　say excited state. COLFORD follows him.

DE LEVIS. Well, General Canynge! It's a little too strong all this--
a little too strong. [Under emotion his voice is slightly more exotic].

CANYNGE. [Calmly] It is obvious, Mr De Levis, that you and Captain Dancy can't both remain members of this Club. We ask you for an explanation before requesting one resignation or the other.

DE LEVIS. You've let me down.

CANYNGE. What!

DE LEVIS. Well, I shall tell people that you and Lord St Erth backed me up for one Club, and asked me to resign from another.

CANYNGE. It's a matter of indifference to me, sir, what you tell people.

ST ERTH. [Drily] You seem a venomous young man.

DE LEVIS. I'll tell you what seems to me venomous, my lord--chasing a man like a pack of hounds because he isn't your breed.

CANYNGE. You appear to have your breed on the brain, sir. Nobody else does, so far as I know.

DE LEVIS. Suppose I had robbed Dancy, would you chase him out for complaining of it?

COLFORD. My God! If you repeat that--

CANYNGE. Steady, Colford!

WINSOR. You make this accusation that Dancy stole your money in my house on no proof--no proof; and you expect Dancy's friends to treat you as if you were a gentleman! That's too strong, if you like!

DE LEVIS. No proof? Bentman told me at Newmarket yesterday that Dancy did know of the sale. He told Goole, and Goole says that he himself spoke of it to Dancy.

WINSOR. Well--if he did?

DE LEVIS. Dancy told you he didn't know of it in General Canynge's presence, and mine. [To CANYNGE] You can't deny that, if you want to.

CANYNGE. Choose your expressions more nicely, please!

DE LEVIS. Proof! Did they find any footmarks in the grounds below that torn creeper? Not a sign! You saw how he can jump; he won ten pounds from me that same evening betting on what he knew was a certainty. That's your Dancy--a common sharper!

CANYNGE. [Nodding towards the billiard-room] Are those fellows still in there, Colford?

COLFORD. Yes.

CANYNGE. Then bring Dancy up, will you? But don't say anything to him.

COLFORD. [To DE LEVIS] You may think yourself damned lucky if he doesn't break your neck.

> He goes out. The three who are left with DE LEVIS avert their eyes from him.

DE LEVIS. [Smouldering] I have a memory, and a sting too. Yes, my lord--since you are good enough to call me venomous. [To CANYNGE] I quite understand--I'm marked for Coventry now, whatever happens. Well, I'll take Dancy with me.

ST ERTH. [To himself] This Club has always had a decent, quiet name.

WINSOR. Are you going to retract, and apologise in front of Dancy and the members who heard you?

DE LEVIS. No fear!

ST ERTH. You must be a very rich man, sir. A jury is likely to take the view that money can hardly compensate for an accusation of that sort.

DE LEVIS stands silent. CANYNGE. Courts of law require proof.

ST ERTH. He can make it a criminal action.

WINSOR. Unless you stop this at once, you may find yourself in prison.
If you can stop it, that is.

ST ERTH. If I were young Dancy, nothing should induce me.

DE LEVIS. But you didn't steal my money, Lord St Erth.

ST ERTH. You're deuced positive, sir. So far as I could understand it,
there were a dozen ways you could have been robbed. It seems to me you
value other men's reputations very lightly.

DE LEVIS. Confront me with Dancy and give me fair play.

WINSOR. [Aside to CANYNGE] Is it fair to Dancy not to let him know?

CANYNGE.   Our duty is to the Club now, WINSOR.   We must have this
cleared
up.

COLFORD comes in, followed by BORRING and DANCY.

ST ERTH. Captain Dancy, a serious accusation has been made against you
by this gentleman in the presence of several members of the Club.

DANCY. What is it?

ST ERTH. That you robbed him of that money at WINSOR's.

DANCY. [Hard and tense] Indeed! On what grounds is he good enough to say that?

DE LEVIS. [Tense too] You gave me that filly to save yourself her keep, and you've been mad about it ever since; you knew from Goole that I had sold her to Kentman and been paid in cash, yet I heard you myself deny that you knew it. You had the next room to me, and you can jump like a cat, as we saw that evening; I found some creepers crushed by a weight on my balcony on that side. When I went to the bath your door was open, and when I came back it was shut.

CANYNGE. That's the first we have heard about the door.

DE LEVIS. I remembered it afterwards.

ST ERTH. Well, Dancy?

DANCY. [With intense deliberation] I'll settle this matter with any weapons, when and where he likes.

ST ERTH. [Drily] It can't be settled that way--you know very well. You must take it to the Courts, unless he retracts.

DANCY. Will you retract?

DE LEVIS. Why did you tell General Canynge you didn't know Kentman had paid me in cash?

DANCY. Because I didn't.

DE LEVIS. Then Kentman and Goole lied--for no reason?

DANCY. That's nothing to do with me.

DE LEVIS. If you were downstairs all the time, as you say, why was your door first open and then shut?

DANCY. Being downstairs, how should I know? The wind, probably.

DE LEVIS. I should like to hear what your wife says about it.

DANCY. Leave my wife alone, you damned Jew!

ST ERTH. Captain Dancy!

DE LEVIS. [White with rage] Thief!

DANCY. Will you fight?

DE LEVIS. You're very smart-dead men tell no tales. No! Bring your action, and we shall see.

DANCY takes a step towards him, but CANYNGE and WINSOR interpose.

ST ERTH. That'll do, Mr De Levis; we won't keep you. [He looks round] Kindly consider your membership suspended till this matter has been threshed out.

DE LEVIS. [Tremulous with anger] Don't trouble yourselves about my membership. I resign it. [To DANCY] You called me a damned Jew. My race was old when you were all savages. I am proud to be a Jew. Au revoir, in the Courts.

He goes out, and silence follows his departure.

ST ERTH. Well, Captain Dancy?

DANCY. If the brute won't fight, what am I to do, sir?

ST ERTH. We've told you--take action, to clear your name.

DANCY. Colford, you saw me in the hall writing letters after our game.

COLFORD. Certainly I did; you were there when I went to the smoking-room.

CANYNGE. How long after you left the billiard-room?

COLFORD. About five minutes.

DANCY. It's impossible for me to prove that I was there all the time.

CANYNGE. It's for De Levis to prove what he asserts. You heard what he said about Goole?

DANCY. If he told me, I didn't take it in.

ST ERTH. This concerns the honour of the Club. Are you going to take action?

DANCY. [Slowly] That is a very expensive business, Lord St Erth, and I'm hard up. I must think it over. [He looks round from face to face] Am I to take it that there is a doubt in your minds, gentlemen?

COLFORD. [Emphatically] No.

CANYNGE. That's not the question, Dancy. This accusation was overheard by various members, and we represent the Club. If you don't take action, judgment will naturally go by default.

DANCY. I might prefer to look on the whole thing as beneath contempt.

He turns and goes out. When he is gone there is an even longer silence than after DE LEVIS's departure.

ST ERTH. [Abruptly] I don't like it.

WINSOR. I've known him all his life.

COLFORD. You may have my head if he did it, Lord St Erth. He and I have been in too many holes together. By Gad! My toe itches for that fellow's butt end.

BORRING. I'm sorry; but has he t-taken it in quite the right way? I should have thought--hearing it s-suddenly--

COLFORD. Bosh!

WINSOR. It's perfectly damnable for him.

ST ERTH. More damnable if he did it, WINSOR.

BORRING. The Courts are b-beastly distrustful, don't you know.

COLFORD. His word's good enough for me.

CANYNGE. We're as anxious to believe Dancy as you, Colford, for the honour of the Army and the Club.

WINSOR. Of course, he'll bring a case, when he's thought it over.

ST ERTH. What are we to do in the meantime?

COLFORD. If Dancy's asked to resign, you may take my resignation too.

BORRING. I thought his wanting to f-fight him a bit screeny.

COLFORD. Wouldn't you have wanted a shot at the brute? A law court? Pah!

WINSOR. Yes. What'll be his position even if he wins?

BORRING. Damages, and a stain on his c-character.

WINSOR. Quite so, unless they find the real thief. People always believe the worst.

COLFORD. [Glaring at BORRING] They do.

CANYNGE. There is no decent way out of a thing of this sort.

ST ERTH. No. [Rising] It leaves a bad taste. I'm sorry for young Mrs Dancy--poor woman!

BORRING. Are you going to play any more?

ST ERTH. [Abruptly] No, sir. Good night to you. Canynge, can I give you a lift?

    He goes out, followed by CANYNGE. BORRING.

[After a slight pause] Well, I shall go and take the t-temperature of the Club.

    He goes out.

COLFORD. Damn that effeminate stammering chap! What can we do for Dancy, WINSOR?

WINSOR. Colford! [A slight pause] The General felt his coat sleeve that night, and it was wet.

COLFORD. Well! What proof's that? No, by George! An old school-fellow, a brother officer, and a pal.

WINSOR. If he did do it--

COLFORD. He didn't. But if he did, I'd stick to him, and see him through it, if I could.

> WINSOR walks over to the fire, stares into it, turns round and stares at COLFORD, who is standing motionless.

COLFORD. Yes, by God!

CURTAIN.

SCENE II

> [NOTE.--This should be a small set capable of being set quickly within that of the previous scene.]

> Morning of the following day. The DANCYS' flat. In the sitting-room of this small abode MABEL DANCY and MARGARET ORME are sitting full face to the audience, on a couch in the centre of the room, in front of the imaginary window. There is a fireplace, Left, with fire burning; a door below it, Left; and a

door on the Right, facing the audience, leads to a corridor and
the outer door of the flat, which is visible. Their voices are
heard in rapid exchange; then as the curtain rises, so does
MABEL.

MABEL. But it's monstrous!

MARGARET. Of course! [She lights a cigarette and hands the case to
MABEL, who, however, sees nothing but her own thoughts] De Levis might
just as well have pitched on me, except that I can't jump more than six
inches in these skirts.

MABEL. It's wicked! Yesterday afternoon at the Club, did you say?
Ronny hasn't said a word to me. Why?

MARGARET. [With a long puff of smoke] Doesn't want you bothered.

MABEL. But----Good heavens!----Me!

MARGARET. Haven't you found out, Mabel, that he isn't exactly
communicative? No desperate character is.

MABEL. Ronny?

MARGARET. Gracious! Wives are at a disadvantage, especially early on.
You've never hunted with him, my dear. I have. He takes more sudden
decisions than any man I ever knew. He's taking one now, I'll bet.

MABEL. That beast, De Levis! I was in our room next door all the time.

MARGARET. Was the door into Ronny's dressing-room open?

MABEL. I don't know; I--I think it was.

MARGARET. Well, you can say so in Court any way. Not that it matters. Wives are liars by law.

MABEL. [Staring down at her] What do you mean--Court?

MARGARET. My dear, he'll have to bring an action for defamation of character, or whatever they call it.

MABEL. Were they talking of this last night at the WINSOR's?

MARGARET. Well, you know a dinner-table, Mabel--Scandal is heaven-sent at this time of year.

MABEL. It's terrible, such a thing--terrible!

MARGARET. [Gloomily] If only Ronny weren't known to be so broke.

MABEL. [With her hands to her forehead] I can't realise--I simply can't. If there's a case would it be all right afterwards?

MARGARET. Do you remember St Offert--cards? No, you wouldn't--you were
in high frocks. Well, St Offert got damages, but he also got the hoof, underneath. He lives in Ireland. There isn't the slightest connection, so far as I can see, Mabel, between innocence and reputation. Look at me!

MABEL. We'll fight it tooth and nail!

MARGARET. Mabel, you're pure wool, right through; everybody's sorry for you.

MABEL. It's for him they ought--

MARGARET. [Again handing the cigarette case] Do smoke, old thing.

MABEL takes a cigarette this time, but does not light it.

It isn't altogether simple. General Canynge was there last night. You don't mind my being beastly frank, do you?

MABEL. No. I want it.

MARGARET. Well, he's all for esprit de corps and that. But he was awfully silent.

MABEL. I hate half-hearted friends. Loyalty comes before everything.

MARGARET. Ye-es; but loyalties cut up against each other sometimes, you know.

MABEL. I must see Ronny. D'you mind if I go and try to get him on the telephone?

MARGARET. Rather not.

MABEL goes out by the door Left.

Poor kid!

She curls herself into a corner of the sofa, as if trying to get away from life. The bell rings. MARGARET stirs, gets up, and goes out into the corridor, where she opens the door to LADY ADELA WINSOR, whom she precedes into the sitting-room.

Enter the second murderer! D'you know that child knew nothing?

LADY A. Where is she?

MARGARET. Telephoning. Adela, if there's going to be an action, we shall be witnesses. I shall wear black georgette with an ecru hat. Have you ever given evidence?

LADY A. Never.

MARGARET. It must be too frightfully thrilling.

LADY A. Oh! Why did I ever ask that wretch De Levis? I used to think him pathetic. Meg did you know----Ronald Dancy's coat was wet? The General happened to feel it.

MARGARET. So that's why he was so silent.

LADY A. Yes; and after the scene in the Club yesterday he went to see those bookmakers, and Goole--what a name!--is sure he told Dancy about the sale.

MARGARET. [Suddenly] I don't care. He's my third cousin. Don't you feel you couldn't, Adela?

LADY A. Couldn't--what?

MARGARET. Stand for De Levis against one of ourselves?

LADY A. That's very narrow, Meg.

MARGARET. Oh! I know lots of splendid Jews, and I rather liked little Ferdy; but when it comes to the point--! They all stick together; why shouldn't we? It's in the blood. Open your jugular, and see if you haven't got it.

LADY A. My dear, my great grandmother was a Jewess. I'm very proud of her.

MARGARET. Inoculated. [Stretching herself] Prejudices, Adela--or are they loyalties--I don't know--cris-cross--we all cut each other's throats from the best of motives.

LADY A. Oh! I shall remember that. Delightful! [Holding up a finger] You got it from Bergson, Meg. Isn't he wonderful?

MARGARET. Yes; have you ever read him?

LADY A. Well--No. [Looking at the bedroom door] That poor child! I quite agree. I shall tell every body it's ridiculous. You don't really think Ronald Dancy--?

MARGARET. I don't know, Adela. There are people who simply can't live without danger. I'm rather like that myself. They're all right when they're getting the D.S.O. or shooting man-eaters; but if there's no excitement going, they'll make it--out of sheer craving. I've seen Ronny Dancy do the maddest things for no mortal reason except the risk. He's had a past, you know.

LADY A. Oh! Do tell!

MARGARET. He did splendidly in the war, of course, because it suited him; but--just before--don't you remember--a very queer bit of riding?

LADY A. No.

MARGARET. Most dare-devil thing--but not quite. You must remember--it was awfully talked about. And then, of course, right up to his marriage--[She lights a cigarette.]

LADY A. Meg, you're very tantalising!

MARGARET. A foreign-looking girl--most plummy. Oh! Ronny's got charm --this Mabel child doesn't know in the least what she's got hold of!

LADY A. But they're so fond of each other!

MARGARET. That's the mistake. The General isn't mentioning the coat, is he?

LADY A. Oh, no! It was only to Charles.

    MABEL returns.

MARGARET. Did you get him?

MABEL. No; he's not at Tattersall's, nor at the Club.

    LADY ADELA rises and greets her with an air which suggests
    bereavement.

LADY A. Nobody's going to believe this, my dear.

MABEL. [Looking straight at her] Nobody who does need come here, or trouble to speak to us again.

LADY A. That's what I was afraid of; you're going to be defiant. Now don't! Just be perfectly natural.

MABEL. So easy, isn't it? I could kill anybody who believes such a thing.

MARGARET. You'll want a solicitor, Mabel, Go to old Mr Jacob Twisden.

LADY A. Yes; he's so comforting.

MARGARET. He got my pearls back once--without loss of life. A frightfully good fireside manner. Do get him here, Mabel, and have a heart-to-heart talk, all three of you!

MABEL. [Suddenly] Listen! There's Ronny!

 DANCY comes in.

DANCY. [With a smile] Very good of you to have come.

MARGARET. Yes. We're just going. Oh! Ronny, this is quite too-- [But his face dries her up; and sidling past, she goes].

LADY A. Charles sent his-love--[Her voice dwindles on the word, and she, too, goes].

DANCY. [Crossing to his wife] What have they been saying?

MABEL. Ronny! Why didn't you tell me?

DANCY. I wanted to see De Levis again first.

MABEL. That wretch! How dare he? Darling! [She suddenly clasps and kisses him. He does not return the kiss, but remains rigid in her arms, so that she draws away and looks at him] It's hurt you awfully, I know.

DANCY. Look here, Mabel! Apart from that muck--this is a ghastly tame-cat sort of life. Let's cut it and get out to Nairobi. I can scare up the money for that.

MABEL. [Aghast] But how can we? Everybody would say--

RONNY. Let them! We shan't be here.

MABEL. I couldn't bear people to think--

DANCY. I don't care a damn what people think monkeys and cats. I never could stand their rotten menagerie. Besides, what does it matter how I act; if I bring an action and get damages--if I pound him to a jelly-- it's all no good! I can't prove it. There'll be plenty of people unconvinced.

MABEL. But they'll find the real thief.

DANCY. [With a queer little smile] Will staying here help them to do that?

MABEL. [In a sort of agony] Oh! I couldn't--it looks like running away. We must stay and fight it!

DANCY. Suppose I didn't get a verdict--you never can tell.

MABEL. But you must--I was there all the time, with the door open.

DANCY. Was it?

MABEL. I'm almost sure.

DANCY. Yes. But you're my wife.

MABEL. [Bewildered] Ronny, I don't understand--suppose I'd been accused of stealing pearls!

DANCY. [Wincing] I can't.

MABEL. But I might--just as easily. What would you think of me if I ran away from it?

DANCY. I see. [A pause] All right! You shall have a run for your money. I'll go and see old Twisden.

MABEL. Let me come! [DANCY shakes his head] Why not? I can't be happy a moment unless I'm fighting this.

DANCY puts out his hand suddenly and grips hers.

DANCY. You are a little brick!

MABEL. [Pressing his hand to her breast and looking into his face] Do you know what Margaret called you?

RONNY. No.

MABEL. A desperate character.

DANCY. Ha! I'm not a tame cat, any more than she.

The bell rings. MABEL goes out to the door and her voice is heard saying coldly.

MABEL. Will you wait a minute, please? Returning. It's De Levis--to see you. [In a low voice] Let me see him alone first. Just for a minute! Do!

DANCY. [After a moment's silence] Go ahead! He goes out into the bedroom.

MABEL. [Going to the door, Right] Come in.

DE LEVIS comes in, and stands embarrassed.

Yes?

DE LEVIS. [With a slight bow] Your husband, Mrs Dancy?

MABEL. He is in. Why do you want to see him?

DE LEVIS. He came round to my rooms just now, when I was out. He threatened me yesterday. I don't choose him to suppose I'm afraid of him.

MABEL. [With a great and manifest effort at self-control] Mr De Levis, you are robbing my husband of his good name.

DE LEVIS. [Sincerely] I admire your trustfulness, Mrs Dancy.

MABEL. [Staring at him] How can you do it? What do you want? What's your motive? You can't possibly believe that my husband is a thief!

DE LEVIS. Unfortunately.

MABEL. How dare you? How dare you? Don't you know that I was in our bedroom all the time with the door open? Do you accuse me too?

DE LEVIS. No, Mrs Dancy.

MABEL. But you do. I must have seen, I must have heard.

DE LEVIS. A wife's memory is not very good when her husband is in danger.

MABEL. In other words, I'm lying.

DE LEVIS. No. Your wish is mother to your thought, that's all.

MABEL. [After staring again with a sort of horror, turns to get control of herself. Then turning back to him] Mr De Levis, I appeal to you as a gentleman to behave to us as you would we should behave to you. Withdraw this wicked charge, and write an apology that Ronald can show.

DE LEVIS. Mrs Dancy, I am not a gentleman, I am only a--damned Jew. Yesterday I might possibly have withdrawn to spare you. But when my race is insulted I have nothing to say to your husband, but as he wishes to see me, I've come. Please let him know.

MABEL. [Regarding him again with that look of horror--slowly] I think what you are doing is too horrible for words.

    DE LEVIS gives her a slight bow, and as he does so DANCY comes quickly in, Left. The two men stand with the length of the sofa between them. MABEL, behind the sofa, turns her eyes on her husband, who has a paper in his right hand.

DE LEVIS. You came to see me.

DANCY. Yes. I want you to sign this.

DE LEVIS. I will sign nothing.

DANCY. Let me read it: "I apologise to Captain Dancy for the reckless and monstrous charge I made against him, and I retract every word of it."

DE LEVIS. Not much!

DANCY. You will sign.

DE LEVIS. I tell you this is useless. I will sign nothing. The charge is true; you wouldn't be playing this game if it weren't. I'm going. You'll hardly try violence in the presence of your wife; and if you try it anywhere else--look out for yourself.

DANCY. Mabel, I want to speak to him alone.

MABEL. No, no!

DE LEVIS. Quite right, Mrs Dancy. Black and tan swashbuckling will only make things worse for him.

DANCY. So you shelter behind a woman, do you, you skulking cur!

> DE LEVIS takes a step, with fists clenched and eyes blazing. DANCY, too, stands ready to spring--the moment is cut short by MABEL going quickly to her husband.

MABEL. Don't, Ronny. It's undignified! He isn't worth it.

> DANCY suddenly tears the paper in two, and flings it into the fire.

DANCY. Get out of here, you swine!

> DE LEVIS stands a moment irresolute, then, turning to the door, he

opens it, stands again for a moment with a smile on his face, then goes. MABEL crosses swiftly to the door, and shuts it as the outer door closes. Then she stands quite still, looking at her husband --her face expressing a sort of startled suspense.

DANCY. [Turning and looking at her] Well! Do you agree with him?

MABEL. What do you mean?

DANCY. That I wouldn't be playing this game unless--

MABEL. Don't! You hurt me!

DANCY. Yes. You don't know much of me, Mabel.

MABEL. Ronny!

DANCY. What did you say to that swine?

MABEL. [Her face averted] That he was robbing us. [Turning to him suddenly] Ronny--you--didn't? I'd rather know.

DANCY. Ha! I thought that was coming.

MABEL. [Covering her face] Oh! How horrible of me--how horrible!

DANCY. Not at all. The thing looks bad.

MABEL. [Dropping her hands] If I can't believe in you, who can? [Going to him, throwing her arms round him, and looking up into his face] Ronny! If all the world--I'd believe in you. You know I would.

DANCY. That's all right, Mabs! That's all right! [His face, above her head, is contorted for a moment, then hardens into a mask] Well, what shall we do? Let's go to that lawyer--let's go--

MABEL. Oh! at once!

DANCY. All right. Get your hat on.

MABEL passes him, and goes into the bedroom, Left. DANCY, left alone, stands quite still, staring before him. With a sudden shrug of his shoulders he moves quickly to his hat and takes it up just as MABEL returns, ready to go out. He opens the door; and crossing him, she stops in the doorway, looking up with a clear and trustful gaze as

The CURTAIN falls.

ACT III

SCENE I

Three months later. Old MR JACOB TWISDEN's Room, at the offices of Twisden & Graviter, in Lincoln's Inn Fields, is spacious, with two large windows at back, a fine old fireplace, Right, a door below it, and two doors, Left. Between the windows is a large table sideways to the window wall, with a chair in the middle on the right-hand side, a chair against the wall, and a client's chair on the left-hand side.

GRAVITER, TWISDEN'S much younger partner, is standing in front of the right-hand window looking out on to the Fields, where the lamps are being lighted, and a taxi's engine is running down below. He turns his sanguine, shrewd face from the window towards a grandfather dock, between the doors, Left, which is striking "four." The door, Left Forward, is opened.

YOUNG CLERK. [Entering] A Mr Gilman, sir, to see Mr Twisden.

GRAVITER. By appointment?

YOUNG CLERK. No, sir. But important, he says.

GRAVITER. I'll see him.

The CLERK goes. GRAVITER sits right of table. The CLERK returns, ushering in an oldish MAN, who looks what he is, the proprietor of a large modern grocery store. He wears a dark overcoat and carries a pot hat. His gingery-grey moustache and mutton-chop whiskers give him the expression of a cat.

GRAVITER. [Sizing up his social standing] Mr Gilman? Yes.

GILMAN. [Doubtfully] Mr Jacob Twisden?

GRAVITER. [Smiling] His partner. Graviter my name is.

GILMAN. Mr Twisden's not in, then?

GRAVITER. No. He's at the Courts. They're just up; he should be in directly. But he'll be busy.

GILMAN. Old Mr Jacob Twisden--I've heard of him.

GRAVITER. Most people have.

GILMAN. It's this Dancy-De Levis case that's keepin' him at the Courts, I suppose?

GRAVITER nods.

Won't be finished for a day or two?

GRAVITER shakes his head. No.

Astonishin' the interest taken in it.

GRAVITER. As you say.

GILMAN. The Smart Set, eh? This Captain Dancy got the D.S.O., didn't he?

GRAVITER nods.

Sad to have a thing like that said about you. I thought he gave his evidence well; and his wife too. Looks as if this De Levis had got some private spite. Searchy la femme, I said to Mrs Gilman only this morning, before I--

GRAVITER. By the way, sir, what is your business?

GILMAN. Well, my business here--No, if you'll excuse me, I'd rather wait and see old Mr Jacob Twisden. It's delicate, and I'd like his experience.

GRAVITER. [With a shrug] Very well; then, perhaps, you'll go in there.

[He moves towards the door, Left Back].

GILMAN. Thank you. [Following] You see, I've never been mixed up with the law--

GRAVITER. [Opening the door] No?

GILMAN. And I don't want to begin. When you do, you don't know where you'll stop, do you? You see, I've only come from a sense of duty; and --other reasons.

GRAVITER. Not uncommon.

GILMAN. [Producing card] This is my card. Gilman's--several branches, but this is the 'ead.

GRAVITER. [Scrutinising card] Exactly.

GILMAN. Grocery--I daresay you know me; or your wife does. They say old Mr Jacob Twisden refused a knighthood. If it's not a rude question, why was that?

GRAVITER. Ask him, sir; ask him.

GILMAN. I said to my wife at the time, "He's holdin' out for a baronetcy."

    GRAVITER Closes the door with an exasperated smile.

YOUNG CLERK. [Opening the door, Left Forward] Mr WINSOR, sir, and Miss
Orme.

They enter, and the CLERK withdraws.

GRAVITER. How d'you do, Miss Orme? How do you do, WINSOR?

WINSOR. Twisden not back, Graviter?

GRAVITER. Not yet.

WINSOR. Well, they've got through De Levis's witnesses. Sir Frederick was at the very top of his form. It's looking quite well. But I hear they've just subpoenaed Canynge after all. His evidence is to be taken to-morrow.

GRAVITER. Oho!

WINSOR. I said Dancy ought to have called him.

GRAVITER. We considered it. Sir Frederic decided that he could use him better in cross-examination.

WINSOR. Well! I don't know that. Can I go and see him before he gives evidence to-morrow?

GRAVITER. I should like to hear Mr Jacob on that, WINSOR. He'll be in directly.

WINSOR. They had Kentman, and Goole, the Inspector, the other bobby, my footman, Dancy's banker, and his tailor.

GRAVITER. Did we shake Kentman or Goole?

WINSOR. Very little. Oh! by the way, the numbers of those two notes were given, and I see they're published in the evening papers. I suppose the police wanted that. I tell you what I find, Graviter--a general feeling that there's something behind it all that doesn't come out.

GRAVITER. The public wants it's money's worth--always does in these Society cases; they brew so long beforehand, you see.

WINSOR. They're looking for something lurid.

MARGARET. When I was in the bog, I thought they were looking for me. [Taking out her cigarette case] I suppose I mustn't smoke, Mr Graviter?

GRAVITER. Do!

MARGARET. Won't Mr Jacob have a fit?

GRAVITER. Yes, but not till you've gone.

MARGARET. Just a whiff. [She lights a cigarette].

WINSOR. [Suddenly] It's becoming a sort of Dreyfus case--people taking sides quite outside the evidence.

MARGARET. There are more of the chosen in Court every day. Mr Graviter, have you noticed the two on the jury?

GRAVITER. [With a smile] No; I can't say--

MARGARET. Oh! but quite distinctly. Don't you think they ought to have been challenged?

GRAVITER. De Levis might have challenged the other ten, Miss Orme.

MARGARET. Dear me, now! I never thought of that.

As she speaks, the door Left Forward is opened and old MR JACOB TWISDEN comes in. He is tallish and narrow, sixty-eight years old, grey, with narrow little whiskers curling round his narrow ears, and a narrow bow-ribbon curling round his collar. He wears a long, narrow-tailed coat, and strapped trousers on his narrow legs. His nose and face are narrow, shrewd, and kindly. He has a way of narrowing his shrewd and kindly eyes. His nose is seen to twitch and snig.

TWISDEN. Ah! How are you, Charles? How do you do, my dear?

MARGARET. Dear Mr Jacob, I'm smoking. Isn't it disgusting? But they don't allow it in Court, you know. Such a pity! The Judge might have a hookah. Oh! wouldn't he look sweet--the darling!

TWISDEN. [With a little, old-fashioned bow] It does not become everybody as it becomes you, Margaret.

MARGARET. Mr Jacob, how charming! [With a slight grimace she puts out her cigarette].

GRAVITER. Man called Gilman waiting in there to see you specially.

TWISDEN. Directly. Turn up the light, would you, Graviter?

GRAVITER. [Turning up the light] Excuse me.

He goes.

WINSOR. Look here, Mr Twisden--

TWISDEN. Sit down; sit down, my dear.

And he himself sits behind the table, as a cup of tea is brought in
to him by the YOUNG CLERK, with two Marie biscuits in the saucer.

Will you have some, Margaret?

MARGARET. No, dear Mr Jacob.

TWISDEN. Charles?

WINSOR. No, thanks. The door is closed.

TWISDEN. [Dipping a biscuit in the tea] Now, then?

WINSOR. The General knows something which on the face of it looks rather
queer. Now that he's going to be called, oughtn't Dancy to be told of
it, so that he may be ready with his explanation, in case it comes out?

TWISDEN. [Pouring some tea into the saucer] Without knowing, I can't
tell you.

     WINSOR and MARGARET exchange looks, and TWISDEN drinks from
the
     saucer. MARGARET. Tell him, Charles.

WINSOR. Well! It rained that evening at Meldon. The General happened
to put his hand on Dancy's shoulder, and it was damp.

     TWISDEN puts the saucer down and replaces the cup in it. They both
     look intently at him.

TWISDEN. I take it that General Canynge won't say anything he's not
compelled to say.

MARGARET. No, of course; but, Mr Jacob, they might ask; they know it rained. And he is such a George Washington.

TWISDEN. [Toying with a pair of tortoise-shell glasses] They didn't ask either of you. Still-no harm in your telling Dancy.

WINSOR. I'd rather you did it, Margaret.

MARGARET. I daresay. [She mechanically takes out her cigarette-case, catches the lift of TWISDEN'S eyebrows, and puts it back].

WINSOR. Well, we'll go together. I don't want Mrs Dancy to hear.

MARGARET. Do tell me, Mr Jacob; is he going to win?

TWISDEN. I think so, Margaret; I think so.

MARGARET. It'll be too--frightful if he doesn't get a verdict, after all this. But I don't know what we shall do when it's over. I've been sitting in that Court all these three days, watching, and it's made me feel there's nothing we like better than seeing people skinned. Well, bye-bye, bless you!

TWISDEN rises and pats her hand.

WINSOR. Half a second, Margaret. Wait for me. She nods and goes out. Mr Twisden, what do you really think?

TWISDEN. I am Dancy's lawyer, my dear Charles, as well as yours.

WINSOR. Well, can I go and see Canynge?

TWISDEN. Better not.

WINSOR. If they get that out of him, and recall me, am I to say he told me of it at the time?

TWISDEN. You didn't feel the coat yourself? And Dancy wasn't present? Then what Canynge told you is not evidence--he'll stop your being asked.

WINSOR. Thank goodness. Good-bye!

>   WINSOR goes out.

>   TWISDEN, behind his table, motionless, taps his teeth with the eyeglasses in his narrow, well-kept hand. After a long shake of his head and a shrug of his rather high shoulders he snips, goes to the window and opens it. Then crossing to the door, Left Back, he throws it open and says

TWISDEN. At your service, sir.

>   GILMAN comes forth, nursing his pot hat.

Be seated.

>   TWISDEN closes the window behind him, and takes his seat.

GILMAN. [Taking the client's chair, to the left of the table] Mr Twisden, I believe? My name's Gilman, head of Gilman's Department Stores. You have my card.

TWISDEN. [Looking at the card] Yes. What can we do for you?

GILMAN. Well, I've come to you from a sense of duty, sir, and also a feelin' of embarrassment. [He takes from his breast pocket an evening paper] You see, I've been followin' this Dancy case--it's a good deal talked of in Putney--and I read this at half-past two this afternoon. To be precise, at 2.25. [He rises and hands the paper to TWISDEN, and with a thick gloved forefinger indicates a passage] When I read these numbers, I 'appened to remember givin' change for a fifty-pound note--don't often 'ave one in, you know--so I went to the cash-box out of curiosity, to see that I 'adn't got it. Well, I 'ad; and here it is. [He draws out from his breast pocket and lays before TWISDEN a fifty-pound banknote] It was brought in to change by a customer of mine three days ago, and he got value for it. Now, that's a stolen note, it seems, and you'd like to know what I did. Mind you, that customer of mine I've known 'im--well--eight or nine years; an Italian he is--wine salesman, and so far's I know, a respectable man-foreign-lookin', but nothin' more. Now, this was at 'alf-past two, and I was at my head branch at Putney, where I live. I want you to mark the time, so as you'll see I 'aven't wasted a minute. I took a cab and I drove straight to my customer's private residence in Putney, where he lives with his daughter--Ricardos his name is, Paolio Ricardos. They tell me there that he's at his business shop in the City. So off I go in the cab again, and there I find him. Well, sir, I showed this paper to him and I produced the note. "Here," I said, "you brought this to me and you got value for it." Well, that man was taken aback. If I'm a judge, Mr Twisden, he was taken aback, not to speak in a guilty way, but he was, as you might say, flummoxed. "Now," I said to him, "where did you get it--that's the point?" He took his time to answer, and then he said: "Well, Mr Gilman," he said, "you know me; I am an honourable man. I can't tell you offhand, but I am above the board." He's foreign, you know, in his expressions. "Yes," I said, "that's all very well," I said, "but here I've got a stolen note and you've got the value for it. Now I tell you," I said, "what I'm going to do; I'm going straight with this note to Mr Jacob Twisden, who's got this Dancy-De Levis case in 'and. He's a well-known Society lawyer," I said, "of great experience." "Oh!" he said, "that is what you do?"--funny the way he

speaks! "Then I come with you!"--And I've got him in the cab below.
I want to tell you everything before he comes up. On the way I tried to
get something out of him, but I couldn't--I could not. "This is very
awkward," I said at last. "It is, Mr Gilman," was his reply; and he
began to talk about his Sicilian claret--a very good wine, mind you; but
under the circumstances it seemed to me uncalled for. Have I made it
clear to you?

TWISDEN. [Who has listened with extreme attention] Perfectly, Mr Gilman.
I'll send down for him. [He touches a hand-bell].

> The YOUNG CLERK appears at the door, Left Forward.

A gentleman in a taxi-waiting. Ask him to be so good as to step up. Oh!
and send Mr Graviter here again.

> The YOUNG CLERK goes out.

GILMAN. As I told you, sir, I've been followin' this case. It's what
you might call piquant. And I should be very glad if it came about that
this helped Captain Dancy. I take an interest, because, to tell you the
truth, [Confidentially] I don't like--well, not to put too fine a point
upon it 'Ebrews. They work harder; they're more sober; they're honest;
and they're everywhere. I've nothing against them, but the fact is--they
get on so.

TWISDEN. [Cocking an eye] A thorn in the flesh, Mr Gilman.

GILMAN. Well, I prefer my own countrymen, and that's the truth of it.

> As he speaks, GRAVITER comes in by the door Left Forward.

TWISDEN. [Pointing to the newspaper and the note] Mr Gilman has brought this, of which he is holder for value. His customer, who changed it three days ago, is coming up.

GRAVITER. The fifty-pounder. I see. [His face is long and reflective].

YOUNG CLERK. [Entering] Mr Ricardos, sir.

    He goes out. RICARDOS is a personable, Italian-looking man in a frock coat, with a dark moustachioed face and dark hair a little grizzled. He looks anxious, and bows.

TWISDEN. Mr Ricardos? My name is Jacob Twisden. My partner. [Holding up a finger, as RICARDOS would speak] Mr Gilman has told us about this note. You took it to him, he says, three days ago; that is, on Monday, and received cash for it?

RICARDOS. Yes, sare.

TWISDEN. You were not aware that it was stolen?

RICARDOS. [With his hand to his breast] Oh! no, sare.

TWISDEN. You received it from--?

RICARDOS. A minute, sare; I would weesh to explain--[With an expressive shrug] in private.

TWISDEN. [Nodding] Mr Gilman, your conduct has been most prompt. You may safely leave the matter in our hands, now. Kindly let us retain this note; and ask for my cashier as you go out and give him [He writes] this. He will reimburse you. We will take any necessary steps ourselves.

GILMAN. [In slight surprise, with modest pride] Well, sir, I'm in your 'ands. I must be guided by you, with your experience. I'm glad you think I acted rightly.

TWISDEN. Very rightly, Mr Gilman--very rightly. [Rising] Good afternoon!

GILMAN. Good afternoon, sir. Good afternoon, gentlemen! [To TWISDEN] I'm sure I'm very 'appy to have made your acquaintance, sir. It's a well-known name.

TWISDEN. Thank you.

GILMAN retreats, glances at RICARDOS, and turns again.

GILMAN. I suppose there's nothing else I ought to do, in the interests of the law? I'm a careful man.

TWISDEN. If there is, Mr Gilman, we will let you know. We have your address. You may make your mind easy; but don't speak of this. It might interfere with Justice.

GILMAN. Oh! I shouldn't dream of it. I've no wish to be mixed up in anything conspicuous. That's not my principle at all. Good-day, gentlemen.

He goes.

TWISDEN. [Seating himself] Now, sir, will you sit down.

But RICARDOS does not sit; he stands looking uneasily across the table at GRAVITER.

You may speak out.

RICARDOS. Well, Mr Tweesden and sare, this matter is very serious for me, and very delicate--it concairns my honour. I am in a great difficulty.

TWISDEN. When in difficulty--complete frankness, sir.

RICARDOS. It is a family matter, sare, I--

TWISDEN. Let me be frank with you. [Telling his points off on his fingers] We have your admission that you changed this stopped note for value. It will be our duty to inform the Bank of England that it has been traced to you. You will have to account to them for your possession of it. I suggest to you that it will be far better to account frankly to us.

RICARDOS. [Taking out a handkerchief and quite openly wiping his hands and forehead] I received this note, sare, with others, from a gentleman, sare, in settlement of a debt of honour, and I know nothing of where he got them.

TWISDEN. H'm! that is very vague. If that is all you can tell us, I'm afraid--

RICARDOS. Gentlemen, this is very painful for me. It is my daughter's good name--[He again wipes his brow].

TWISDEN. Come, sir, speak out!

RICARDOS. [Desperately] The notes were a settlement to her from this gentleman, of whom she was a great friend.

TWISDEN. [Suddenly] I am afraid we must press you for the name of the gentleman.

RICARDOS. Sare, if I give it to you, and it does 'im 'arm, what will my daughter say? This is a bad matter for me. He behaved well to her; and she is attached to him still; sometimes she is crying yet because she lost him. And now we betray him, perhaps, who knows? This is very unpleasant for me. [Taking up the paper] Here it gives the number of another note--a 'undred-pound note. I 'ave that too. [He takes a note from his breast pocket].

GRAVITER. How much did he give you in all?

RICARDOS. For my daughter's settlement one thousand pounds. I understand he did not wish to give a cheque because of his marriage. So I did not think anything about it being in notes, you see.

TWISDEN. When did he give you this money?

RICARDOS. The middle of Octobare last.

TWISDEN. [Suddenly looking up] Mr Ricardos, was it Captain Dancy?

RICARDOS. [Again wiping his forehead] Gentlemen, I am so fond of my daughter. I have only the one, and no wife.

TWISDEN. [With an effort] Yes, yes; but I must know.

RICARDOS. Sare, if I tell you, will you give me your good word that my daughter shall not hear of it?

TWISDEN. So far as we are able to prevent it--certainly.

RICARDOS. Sare, I trust you.--It was Captain Dancy.

A long pause.

GRAVITER [Suddenly] Were you blackmailing him?

TWISDEN. [Holding up his hand] My partner means, did you press him for this settlement?

RICARDOS. I did think it my duty to my daughter to ask that he make compensation to her.

TWISDEN. With threats that you would tell his wife?

RICARDOS. [With a shrug] Captain Dancy was a man of honour. He said: "Of course I will do this." I trusted him. And a month later I did remind him, and he gave me this money for her. I do not know where he got it--I do not know. Gentlemen, I have invested it all on her--every penny-except this note, for which I had the purpose to buy her a necklace. That is the sweared truth.

TWISDEN. I must keep this note. [He touches the hundred-pound note] You will not speak of this to anyone. I may recognise that you were a holder for value received--others might take a different view. Good-day, sir. Graviter, see Mr Ricardos out, and take his address.

RICARDOS. [Pressing his hands over the breast of his frock coat--with a sigh] Gentlemen, I beg you--remember what I said. [With a roll of his eyes] My daughter--I am not happee. Good-day.

He turns and goes out slowly, Left Forward, followed by GRAVITER.

TWISDEN. [To himself] Young Dancy! [He pins the two notes together and places them in an envelope, then stands motionless except for his eyes and hands, which restlessly express the disturbance within him.]

GRAVITER returns, carefully shuts the door, and going up to him, hands him RICARDOS' card.

[Looking at the card] Villa Benvenuto. This will have to be verified, but I'm afraid it's true. That man was not acting.

GRAVITER. What's to be done about Dancy?

TWISDEN. Can you understand a gentleman--?

GRAVITER. I don't know, sir. The war loosened "form" all over the place. I saw plenty of that myself. And some men have no moral sense. From the first I've had doubts.

TWISDEN. We can't go on with the case.

GRAVITER. Phew!... [A moment's silence] Gosh! It's an awful thing for his wife.

TWISDEN. Yes.

GRAVITER [Touching the envelope] Chance brought this here, sir. That man won't talk--he's too scared.

TWISDEN. Gilman.

GRAVITER. Too respectable. If De Levis got those notes back, and the rest of the money, anonymously?

TWISDEN. But the case, Graviter; the case.

GRAVITER. I don't believe this alters what I've been thinking.

TWISDEN. Thought is one thing--knowledge another. There's duty to our profession. Ours is a fine calling. On the good faith of solicitors a very great deal hangs. [He crosses to the hearth as if warmth would help him].

GRAVITER. It'll let him in for a prosecution. He came to us in confidence.

TWISDEN. Not as against the law.

GRAVITER. No. I suppose not. [A pause] By Jove, I don't like losing this case. I don't like the admission we backed such a wrong 'un.

TWISDEN. Impossible to go on. Apart from ourselves, there's Sir Frederic. We must disclose to him--can't let him go on in the dark. Complete confidence between solicitor and counsel is the essence of professional honour.

GRAVITER. What are you going to do then, sir?

TWISDEN. See Dancy at once. Get him on the phone.

GRAVITER. [Taking up the telephone] Get me Captain Dancy's flat.... What?... [To TWISDEN] Mrs Dancy is here. That's a propos with a vengeance. Are you going to see her, sir?

TWISDEN. [After a moment's painful hesitation] I must.

GRAVITER. [Telephoning] Bring Mrs Dancy up. [He turns to the window].

MABEL DANDY is shown in, looking very pale. TWISDEN advances from the fire, and takes her hand.

MABEL. Major Colford's taken Ronny off in his car for the night. I thought it would do him good. I said I'd come round in case there was anything you wanted to say before to-morrow.

TWISDEN. [Taken aback] Where have they gone?

MABEL. I don't know, but he'll be home before ten o'clock to-morrow. Is there anything?

TWISDEN. Well, I'd like to see him before the Court sits. Send him on here as soon as he comes.

MABEL. [With her hand to her forehead] Oh! Mr Twisden, when will it be over? My head's getting awful sitting in that Court.

TWISDEN. My dear Mrs Dancy, there's no need at all for you to come down to-morrow; take a rest and nurse your head.

MABEL. Really and truly?

TWISDEN. Yes; it's the very best thing you can do.

GRAVITER turns his head, and looks at them unobserved.

MABEL. How do you think it's going?

TWISDEN. It went very well to-day; very well indeed.

MABEL. You must be awfully fed up with us.

TWISDEN. My dear young lady, that's our business. [He takes her hand].

MABEL's face suddenly quivers. She draws her hand away, and covers her lips with it.

There, there! You want a day off badly.

MABEL. I'm so tired of--! Thank you so much for all you're doing.
Good night! Good night, Mr Graviter!

GRAVITER. Good night, Mrs Dancy.

MABEL goes.

GRAVITER. D'you know, I believe she knows.

TWISDEN. No, no! She believes in him implicitly. A staunch little woman. Poor thing!

GRAVITER. Hasn't that shaken you, sir? It has me.

TWISDEN. No, no! I--I can't go on with the case. It's breaking faith.
Get Sir Frederic's chambers.

GRAVITER. [Telephoning, and getting a reply, looks round at TWISDEN]
Yes?

TWISDEN. Ask if I can come round and see him.

GRAVITER. [Telephoning] Can Sir Frederic spare Mr Twisden a few minutes now if he comes round? [Receiving reply] He's gone down to Brighton for the night.

TWISDEN. H'm! What hotel?

GRAVITER. [Telephoning] What's his address? What...? [To TWISDEN] The Bedford.

TWISDEN. I'll go down.

GRAVITER. [Telephoning] Thank you. All right. [He rings off].

TWISDEN. Just look out the trains down and up early to-morrow.

GRAVITER takes up an A B C, and TWISDEN takes up the Ricardos card.

TWISDEN. Send to this address in Putney, verify the fact that Ricardos has a daughter, and give me a trunk call to Brighton. Better go yourself, Graviter. If you see her, don't say anything, of course-- invent some excuse. [GRAVITER nods] I'll be up in time to see Dancy.

GRAVITER. By George! I feel bad about this.

TWISDEN. Yes. But professional honour comes first. What time is that train? [He bends over the ABC].

CURTAIN.

SCENE II

The same room on the following morning at ten-twenty-five, by the Grandfather clock.

The YOUNG CLERK is ushering in DANCY, whose face is perceptibly harder than it was three months ago, like that of a man who has lived under great restraint.

DANCY. He wanted to see me before the Court sat.

YOUNG CLERK. Yes, sir. Mr Twisden will see you in one minute. He had to go out of town last night. [He prepares to open the waiting-room door].

DANCY. Were you in the war?

YOUNG CLERK. Yes.

DANCY. How can you stick this?

YOUNG CLERK. [With a smile] My trouble was to stick that, sir.

DANCY. But you get no excitement from year's end to year's end. It'd drive me mad.

YOUNG CLERK. [Shyly] A case like this is pretty exciting. I'd give a lot to see us win it.

DANCY. [Staring at him] Why? What is it to you?

YOUNG CLERK. I don't know, sir. It's--it's like football--you want your side to win. [He opens the waiting-room door. Expanding] You see some rum starts, too, in a lawyer's office in a quiet way.

DANCY enters the waiting-room, and the YOUNG CLERK, shutting the door, meets TWISDEN as he comes in, Left Forward, and takes from him overcoat, top hat, and a small bag.

YOUNG CLERK. Captain Dancy's waiting, sir. [He indicates the waiting-room].

TWISDEN. [Narrowing his lips] Very well. Mr Graviter gone to the Courts?

YOUNG CLERK. Yes, sir.

TWISDEN. Did he leave anything for me?

YOUNG CLERK. On the table, sir.

TWISDEN. [Taking up an envelope] Thank you.

    The CLERK goes.

TWISDEN. [Opening the envelope and reading] "All corroborates." H'm! [He puts it in his pocket and takes out of an envelope the two notes, lays them on the table, and covers them with a sheet of blotting-paper; stands a moment preparing himself, then goes to the door of the waiting-room, opens it, and says:] Now, Captain Dancy. Sorry to have kept you waiting.

DANCY. [Entering] WINSOR came to me yesterday about General Canynge's evidence. Is that what you wanted to speak to me about?

TWISDEN. No. It isn't that.

DANCY. [Looking at his wrist watch] By me it's just on the half-hour, sir.

TWISDEN. Yes. I don't want you to go to the Court.

DANCY. Not?

TWISDEN. I have very serious news for you.

DANCY. [Wincing and collecting himself] Oh!

TWISDEN. These two notes. [He uncovers the notes] After the Court rose
yesterday we had a man called Ricardos here. [A pause] Is there any need
for me to say more?

DANCY. [Unflinching] No. What now?

TWISDEN. Our duty was plain; we could not go on with the case. I have
consulted Sir Frederic. He felt--he felt that he must throw up his
brief, and he will do that the moment the Court sits. Now I want to talk
to you about what you're going to do.

DANCY. That's very good of you, considering.

TWISDEN. I don't pretend to understand, but I imagine you may have done
this in a moment of reckless bravado, feeling, perhaps, that as you gave
the mare to De Levis, the money was by rights as much yours as his.

   Stopping DANCY, who is about to speak, with a gesture.

To satisfy a debt of honour to this--lady; and, no doubt, to save your
wife from hearing of it from the man Ricardos. Is that so?

DANCY. To the life.

TWISDEN. It was mad, Captain Dancy, mad! But the question now is: What do you owe to your wife? She doesn't dream--I suppose?

DANCY. [With a twitching face] No.

TWISDEN. We can't tell what the result of this collapse will be. The police have the theft in hand. They may issue a warrant. The money could be refunded, and the costs paid--somehow that can all be managed. But it may not help. In any case, what end is served by your staying in the country? You can't save your honour--that's gone. You can't save your wife's peace of mind. If she sticks to you--do you think she will?

DANCY. Not if she's wise.

TWISDEN. Better go! There's a war in Morocco.

DANCY. [With a bitter smile] Good old Morocco!

TWISDEN. Will you go, then, at once, and leave me to break it to your wife?

DANCY. I don't know yet.

TWISDEN. You must decide quickly, to catch a boat train. Many a man has made good. You're a fine soldier.

DANCY. There are alternatives.

TWISDEN. Now, go straight from this office. You've a passport, I suppose; you won't need a visa for France, and from there you can find means to slip over. Have you got money on you? [Dancy nods]. We will see what we can do to stop or delay proceedings.

DANCY. It's all damned kind of you. [With difficulty] But I must think of my wife. Give me a few minutes.

TWISDEN. Yes, yes; go in there and think it out.

> He goes to the door, Right, and opens it. DANCY passes him and goes out. TWISDEN rings a bell and stands waiting.

CLERK. [Entering] Yes, sir?

TWISDEN. Tell them to call a taxi.

CLERK. [Who has a startled look] Yes, sir. Mr Graviter has come in, air, with General Canynge. Are you disengaged?

TWISDEN. Yes.

> The CLERK goes out, and almost immediately GRAVITER and CANYNGE enter. Good-morning, General. [To GRAVITER]

Well?

GRAVITER. Sir Frederic got up at once and said that since the publication of the numbers of those notes, information had reached him which forced him to withdraw from the case. Great sensation, of course. I left Bromley in charge. There'll be a formal verdict for the defendant, with costs. Have you told Dancy?

TWISDEN. Yes. He's in there deciding what he'll do.

CANYNGE. [Grave and vexed] This is a dreadful thing, Twisden. I've been afraid of it all along. A soldier! A gallant fellow, too. What on earth got into him?

TWISDEN. There's no end to human nature, General.

GRAVITER. You can see queerer things in the papers, any day.

CANYNGE. That poor young wife of his! WINSOR gave me a message for you,
Twisden. If money's wanted quickly to save proceedings, draw on him.
Is there anything I can do?

TWISDEN. I've advised him to go straight off to Morocco.

CANYNGE. I don't know that an asylum isn't the place for him. He must be off his head at moments. That jump-crazy! He'd have got a verdict on that alone--if they'd seen those balconies. I was looking at them when I was down there last Sunday. Daring thing, Twisden. Very few men, on a dark night--He risked his life twice. That's a shrewd fellow--young De Levis. He spotted Dancy's nature.

 The YOUNG CLERK enters.

CLERK. The taxi's here, sir. Will you see Major Colford and Miss Orme?

TWISDEN. Graviter--No; show them in.

 The YOUNG CLERK goes.

CANYNGE. Colford's badly cut up.

 MARGARET ORME and COLFORD enter.

COLFORD. [Striding forward] There must be some mistake about this, Mr Twisden.

TWISDEN. Hssh! Dancy's in there. He's admitted it.

Voices are subdued at once.

COLFORD. What? [With emotion] If it were my own brother, I couldn't feel it more. But--damn it! What right had that fellow to chuck up the case--without letting him know, too. I came down with Dancy this morning, and he knew nothing about it.

TWISDEN. [Coldly] That was unfortunately unavoidable.

COLFORD. Guilty or not, you ought to have stuck to him--it's not playing the game, Mr Twisden.

TWISDEN. You must allow me to judge where my duty lay, in a very hard case.

COLFORD. I thought a man was safe with his solicitor.

CANYNGE. Colford, you don't understand professional etiquette.

COLFORD. No, thank God!

TWISDEN. When you have been as long in your profession as I have been in mine, Major Colford, you will know that duty to your calling outweighs duty to friend or client.

COLFORD. But I serve the Country.

TWISDEN. And I serve the Law, sir.

CANYNGE. Graviter, give me a sheet of paper. I'll write a letter for him.

MARGARET. [Going up to TWISDEN] Dear Mr Jacob--pay De Levis. You know
my pearls--put them up the spout again. Don't let Ronny be--

TWISDEN. Money isn't the point, Margaret.

MARGARET. It's ghastly! It really is.

COLFORD. I'm going in to shake hands with him. [He starts to cross the room].

TWISDEN. Wait! We want him to go straight off to Morocco. Don't upset him. [To COLFORD and MARGARET] I think you had better go. If, a little later, Margaret, you could go round to Mrs Dancy--

COLFORD. Poor little Mabel Dancy! It's perfect hell for her.

They have not seen that DANCY has opened the door behind them.

DANCY. It is!

They all turn round in consternation.

COLFORD. [With a convulsive movement] Old boy!

DANCY. No good, Colford. [Gazing round at them] Oh! clear out--I can't stand commiseration; and let me have some air.

TWISDEN motions to COLFORD and MARGARET to go; and as he turns to
DANCY, they go out. GRAVITER also moves towards the door. The GENERAL sits motionless. GRAVITER goes Out.

TWISDEN. Well?

DANCY. I'm going home, to clear up things with my wife. General Canynge, I don't quite know why I did the damned thing. But I did, and there's an end of it.

CANYNGE. Dancy, for the honour of the Army, avoid further scandal if you can. I've written a letter to a friend of mine in the Spanish War Office. It will get you a job in their war. [CANYNGE closes the envelope].

DANCY. Very good of you. I don't know if I can make use of it.

    CANYNGE stretches out the letter, which TWISDEN hands to DANCY, who
       takes it. GRAVITER re-opens the door.

TWISDEN. What is it?

GRAVITER. De Levis is here.

TWISDEN. De Levis? Can't see him.

DANCY. Let him in!

    After a moment's hesitation TWISDEN nods, and GRAVITER goes out.
    The three wait in silence with their eyes fixed on the door, the
    GENERAL sitting at the table, TWISDEN by his chair, DANCY between
    him and the door Right. DE LEVIS comes in and shuts the door. He
    is advancing towards TWISDEN when his eyes fall on DANCY, and he
    stops.

TWISDEN. You wanted to see me?

DE LEVIS. [Moistening his lips] Yes. I came to say that--that I overheard--I am afraid a warrant is to be issued. I wanted you to realise--it's not my doing. I'll give it no support. I'm content. I don't want my money. I don't even want costs. Dancy, do you understand?

> DANCY does not answer, but looks at him with nothing alive in his face but his eyes.

TWISDEN. We are obliged to you, Sir. It was good of you to come.

DE LEVIS. [With a sort of darting pride] Don't mistake me. I didn't come because I feel Christian; I am a Jew. I will take no money--not even that which was stolen. Give it to a charity. I'm proved right. And now I'm done with the damned thing. Good-morning!

> He makes a little bow to CANYNGE and TWISDEN, and turns to face DANCY, who has never moved. The two stand motionless, looking at each other, then DE LEVIS shrugs his shoulders and walks out. When he is gone there is a silence.

CANYNGE. [Suddenly] You heard what he said, Dancy. You have no time to lose.

> But DANCY does not stir.

TWISDEN. Captain Dancy?

> Slowly, without turning his head, rather like a man in a dream, DANCY walks across the room, and goes out.

CURTAIN.

SCENE III

The DANCYS' sitting-room, a few minutes later. MABEL DANCY is
sitting alone on the sofa with a newspaper on her lap; she is only
just up, and has a bottle of smelling-salts in her hand. Two or
three other newspapers are dumped on the arm of the sofa. She
topples the one off her lap and takes up another as if she couldn't
keep away from them; drops it in turn, and sits staring before her,
sniffing at the salts. The door, Right, is opened and DANCY comes
in.

MABEL. [Utterly surprised] Ronny! Do they want me in Court?

DANCY. No.

MABEL. What is it, then? Why are you back?

DANCY. Spun.

MABEL. [Blank] Spun? What do you mean? What's spun?

DANCY. The case. They've found out through those notes.

MABEL. Oh! [Staring at his face] Who?

DANCY. Me!

MABEL. [After a moment of horrified stillness] Don't, Ronny! Oh! No!
Don't! [She buries her face in the pillows of the sofa].

DANCY stands looking down at her.

DANCY. Pity you wouldn't come to Africa three months ago.

MABEL. Why didn't you tell me then? I would have gone.

DANCY. You wanted this case. Well, it's fallen down.

MABEL. Oh! Why didn't I face it? But I couldn't--I had to believe.

DANCY. And now you can't. It's the end, Mabel.

MABEL. [Looking up at him] No.

DANCY goes suddenly on his knees and seizes her hand.

DANCY. Forgive me!

MABEL. [Putting her hand on his head] Yes; oh, yes! I think I've known a long time, really. Only--why? What made you?

DANCY. [Getting up and speaking in jerks] It was a crazy thing to do; but, damn it, I was only looting a looter. The money was as much mine as his. A decent chap would have offered me half. You didn't see the brute look at me that night at dinner as much as to say: "You blasted fool!" It made me mad. That wasn't a bad jump-twice over. Nothing in the war took quite such nerve. [Grimly] I rather enjoyed that evening.

MABEL. But--money! To keep it!

DANCY. [Sullenly] Yes, but I had a debt to pay.

MABEL. To a woman?

DANCY. A debt of honour--it wouldn't wait.

MABEL. It was--it was to a woman. Ronny, don't lie any more.

DANCY. [Grimly] Well! I wanted to save your knowing. I'd promised a thousand. I had a letter from her father that morning, threatening to tell you. All the same, if that tyke hadn't jeered at me for parlour tricks!--But what's the good of all this now? [Sullenly] Well--it may cure you of loving me. Get over that, Mab; I never was worth it--and I'm done for!

MABEL. The woman--have you--since--?

DANCY. [Energetically] No! You supplanted her. But if you'd known I was leaving a woman for you, you'd never have married me. [He walks over to the hearth].

> MABEL too gets up. She presses her hands to her forehead, then
> walks blindly round to behind the sofa and stands looking straight
> in front of her.

MABEL. [Coldly] What has happened, exactly?

DANCY. Sir Frederic chucked up the case. I've seen Twisden; they want me to run for it to Morocco.

MABEL. To the war there?

DANCY. Yes. There's to be a warrant out.

MABEL. A prosecution? Prison? Oh, go! Don't wait a minute! Go!

DANCY. Blast them!

MABEL. Oh, Ronny! Please! Please! Think what you'll want. I'll pack. Quick! No! Don't wait to take things. Have you got money?

DANCY. [Nodding] This'll be good-bye, then!

MABEL. [After a moment's struggle] Oh! No! No, no! I'll follow--I'll come out to you there.

DANCY. D'you mean you'll stick to me?

MABEL. Of course I'll stick to you.

DANCY seizes her hand and puts it to his lips. The bell rings.

MABEL. [In terror] Who's that?

> The bell rings again. DANCY moves towards the door.

No! Let me!

> She passes him and steals out to the outer door of the flat, where she stands listening. The bell rings again. She looks through the slit of the letter-box. While she is gone DANCY stands quite still, till she comes back.

MABEL. Through the letter-bog--I can see----It's--it's police. Oh! God!... Ronny! I can't bear it.

DANCY. Heads up, Mab! Don't show the brutes!

MABEL. Whatever happens, I'll go on loving you. If it's prison--I'll wait. Do you understand? I don't care what you did--I don't care! I'm just the same. I will be just the same when you come back to me.

DANCY. [Slowly] That's not in human nature.

MABEL. It is. It's in Me.

DANCY. I've crocked up your life.

MABEL. No, no! Kiss me!

    A long kiss, till the bell again startles them apart, and there is a loud knock.

DANCY. They'll break the door in. It's no good--we must open. Hold them in check a little. I want a minute or two.

MABEL. [Clasping him] Ronny! Oh, Ronny! It won't be for long--I'll be waiting! I'll be waiting--I swear it.

DANCY. Steady, Mab! [Putting her back from him] Now!

    He opens the bedroom door, Left, and stands waiting for her to go. Summoning up her courage, she goes to open the outer door. A sudden change comes over DANCY'S face; from being stony it grows almost maniacal.

DANCY. [Under his breath] No! No! By God! No! He goes out into the bedroom, closing the door behind him.

    MABEL has now opened the outer door, and disclosed INSPECTOR DEDE and the YOUNG CONSTABLE who were summoned to Meldon Court on the

night of the theft, and have been witnesses in the case. Their voices are heard.

MABEL. Yes?

INSPECTOR. Captain Dancy in, madam?

MABEL. I am not quite sure--I don't think so.

INSPECTOR. I wish to speak to him a minute. Stay here, Grover. Now, madam!

MABEL. Will you come in while I see?

She comes in, followed by the INSPECTOR.

INSPECTOR. I should think you must be sure, madam. This is not a big place.

MABEL. He was changing his clothes to go out. I think he has gone.

INSPECTOR. What's that door?

MABEL. To our bedroom.

INSPECTOR. [Moving towards it] He'll be in there, then.

MABEL. What do you want, Inspector?

INSPECTOR. [Melting] Well, madam, it's no use disguising it. I'm exceedingly sorry, but I've a warrant for his arrest.

MABEL. Inspector!

INSPECTOR. I'm sure I've every sympathy for you, madam; but I must carry out my instructions.

MABEL. And break my heart?

INSPECTOR. Well, madam, we're--we're not allowed to take that into consideration. The Law's the Law.

MABEL. Are you married?

INSPECTOR. I am.

MABEL. If you--your wife--

    The INSPECTOR raises his hand, deprecating.

[Speaking low] Just half an hour! Couldn't you? It's two lives--two whole lives! We've only been married four months. Come back in half an hour. It's such a little thing--nobody will know. Nobody. Won't you?

INSPECTOR. Now, madam--you must know my duty.

MABEL. Inspector, I beseech you--just half an hour.

INSPECTOR. No, no--don't you try to undermine me--I'm sorry for you; but don't you try it! [He tries the handle, then knocks at the door].

DANCY'S VOICE. One minute!

INSPECTOR. It's locked. [Sharply] Is there another door to that room? Come, now--

The bell rings.

[Moving towards the door, Left; to the CONSTABLE] Who's that out there?

CONSTABLE. A lady and gentleman, sir.

INSPECTOR. What lady and-- Stand by, Grover!

DANCY'S VOICE. All right! You can come in now.

> There is the noise of a lock being turned. And almost immediately
> the sound of a pistol shot in the bedroom. MABEL rushes to the
> door, tears it open, and disappears within, followed by the
> INSPECTOR, just as MARGARET ORME and COLFORD come in from the
> passage, pursued by the CONSTABLE. They, too, all hurry to the
> bedroom door and disappear for a moment; then COLFORD and MARGA-
RET
> reappear, supporting MABEL, who faints as they lay her on the sofa.
> COLFORD takes from her hand an envelope, and tears it open.

COLFORD. It's addressed to me. [He reads it aloud to MARGARET in a low voice].

"DEAR COLFORD,--This is the only decent thing I can do. It's too damned unfair to her. It's only another jump. A pistol keeps faith. Look after her, Colford--my love to her, and you."

MARGARET gives a sort of choking sob, then, seeing the smelling bottle, she snatches it up, and turns to revive MABEL.

COLFORD. Leave her! The longer she's unconscious, the better.

INSPECTOR. [Re-entering] This is a very serious business, sir.

COLFORD. [Sternly] Yes, Inspector; you've done for my best friend.

INSPECTOR. I, sir? He shot himself.

COLFORD. Hara-kiri.

INSPECTOR. Beg pardon?

COLFORD. [He points with the letter to MABEL] For her sake, and his own.

INSPECTOR. [Putting out his hand] I'll want that, sir.

COLFORD. [Grimly] You shall have it read at the inquest. Till then-- it's addressed to me, and I stick to it.

INSPECTOR. Very well, sir. Do you want to have a look at him?

> COLFORD passes quickly into the bedroom, followed by the INSPECTOR. MARGARET remains kneeling beside MABEL.

> COLFORD comes quickly back. MARGARET looks up at him. He stands very still.

COLFORD. Neatly--through the heart.

MARGARET [wildly] Keeps faith! We've all done that. It's not enough.

COLFORD. [Looking down at MABEL] All right, old boy!

> The CURTAIN falls.

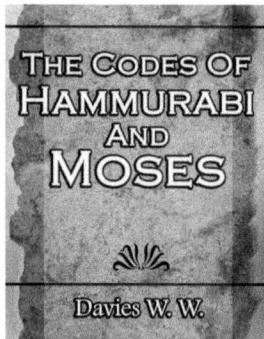

The Codes Of Hammurabi And Moses
W. W. Davies

QTY

The discovery of the Hammurabi Code is one of the greatest achievements of archaeology, and is of paramount interest, not only to the student of the Bible, but also to all those interested in ancient history...

Religion   **ISBN:** *1-59462-338-4*   **Pages:132**
MSRP $12.95

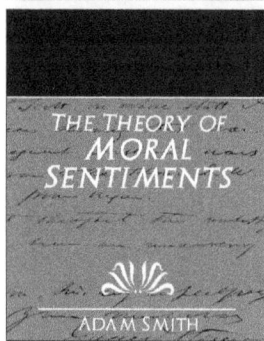

The Theory of Moral Sentiments
Adam Smith

QTY

This work from 1749. contains original theories of conscience amd moral judgment and it is the foundation for systemof morals.

Philosophy   **ISBN:** *1-59462-777-0*   **Pages:536**
MSRP $19.95

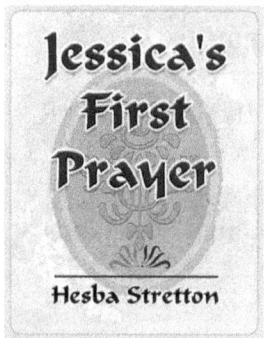

Jessica's First Prayer
Hesba Stretton

QTY

In a screened and secluded corner of one of the many railway-bridges which span the streets of London there could be seen a few years ago, from five o'clock every morning until half past eight, a tidily set-out coffee-stall, consisting of a trestle and board, upon which stood two large tin cans, with a small fire of charcoal burning under each so as to keep the coffee boiling during the early hours of the morning when the work-people were thronging into the city on their way to their daily toil...

Childrens   **ISBN:** *1-59462-373-2*   **Pages:84**
MSRP $9.95

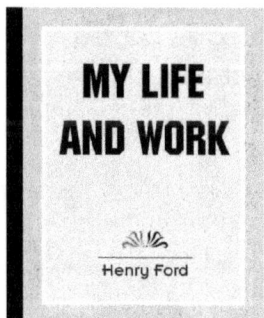

My Life and Work
Henry Ford

QTY

Henry Ford revolutionized the world with his implementation of mass production for the Model T automobile. Gain valuable business insight into his life and work with his own auto-biography... "We have only started on our development of our country we have not as yet, with all our talk of wonderful progress, done more than scratch the surface. The progress has been wonderful enough but..."

Biographies/   **ISBN:** *1-59462-198-5*   **Pages:300**
MSRP $21.95

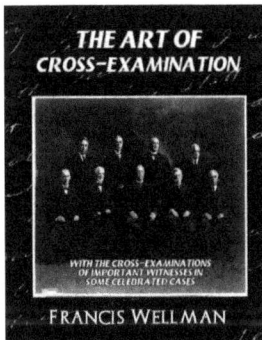

The Art of Cross-Examination
Francis Wellman

QTY

I presume it is the experience of every author, after his first book is published upon an important subject, to be almost overwhelmed with a wealth of ideas and illustrations which could readily have been included in his book, and which to his own mind, at least, seem to make a second edition inevitable. Such certainly was the case with me; and when the first edition had reached its sixth impression in five months, I rejoiced to learn that it seemed to my publishers that the book had met with a sufficiently favorable reception to justify a second and considerably enlarged edition. ..

Pages:412

Reference   ISBN: *1-59462-647-2*   *MSRP $19.95*

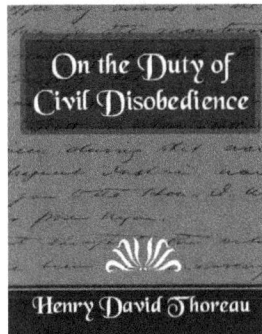

On the Duty of Civil Disobedience
Henry David Thoreau

QTY

Thoreau wrote his famous essay, On the Duty of Civil Disobedience, as a protest against an unjust but popular war and the immoral but popular institution of slave-owning. He did more than write—he declined to pay his taxes, and was hauled off to gaol in consequence. Who can say how much this refusal of his hastened the end of the war and of slavery ?

Law   ISBN: *1-59462-747-9*   **Pages:48**

MSRP $7.45

Dream Psychology Psychoanalysis for Beginners
Sigmund Freud

QTY

Sigmund Freud, born Sigismund Schlomo Freud (May 6, 1856 - September 23, 1939), was a Jewish-Austrian neurologist and psychiatrist who co-founded the psychoanalytic school of psychology. Freud is best known for his theories of the unconscious mind, especially involving the mechanism of repression; his redefinition of sexual desire as mobile and directed towards a wide variety of objects; and his therapeutic techniques, especially his understanding of transference in the therapeutic relationship and the presumed value of dreams as sources of insight into unconscious desires.

Pages:196

Psychology   ISBN: *1-59462-905-6*   *MSRP $15.45*

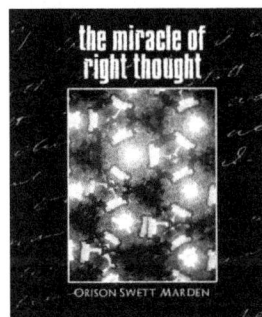

The Miracle of Right Thought
Orison Swett Marden

QTY

Believe with all of your heart that you will do what you were made to do. When the mind has once formed the habit of holding cheerful, happy, prosperous pictures, it will not be easy to form the opposite habit. It does not matter how improbable or how far away this realization may see, or how dark the prospects may be, if we visualize them as best we can, as vividly as possible, hold tenaciously to them and vigorously struggle to attain them, they will gradually become actualized, realized in the life. But a desire, a longing without endeavor, a yearning abandoned or held indifferently will vanish without realization.

Pages:360

Self Help   ISBN: *1-59462-644-8*   *MSRP $25.45*

☐ **The Rosicrucian Cosmo-Conception Mystic Christianity** by *Max Heindel*   ISBN: *1-59462-188-8* **$38.95**
The Rosicrucian Cosmo-conception is not dogmatic, neither does it appeal to any other authority than the reason of the student. It is: not controversial, but is: sent forth in the, hope that it may help to clear...   New Age/Religion Pages 646

☐ **Abandonment To Divine Providence** by *Jean-Pierre de Caussade*   ISBN: *1-59462-228-0* **$25.95**
"The Rev. Jean Pierre de Caussade was one of the most remarkable spiritual writers of the Society of Jesus in France in the 18th Century. His death took place at Toulouse in 1751. His works have gone through many editions and have been republished...   Inspirational/Religion Pages 400

☐ **Mental Chemistry** by *Charles Haanel*   ISBN: *1-59462-192-6* **$23.95**
Mental Chemistry allows the change of material conditions by combining and appropriately utilizing the power of the mind. Much like applied chemistry creates something new and unique out of careful combinations of chemicals the mastery of mental chemistry...   New Age Pages 354

☐ **The Letters of Robert Browning and Elizabeth Barret Barrett 1845-1846 vol II**   ISBN: *1-59462-193-4* **$35.95**
by *Robert Browning* and *Elizabeth Barrett*
     Biographies Pages 596

☐ **Gleanings In Genesis (volume I)** by *Arthur W. Pink*   ISBN: *1-59462-130-6* **$27.45**
Appropriately has Genesis been termed "the seed plot of the Bible" for in it we have, in germ form, almost all of the great doctrines which are afterwards fully developed in the books of Scripture which follow...   Religion/Inspirational Pages 420

☐ **The Master Key** by *L. W. de Laurence*   ISBN: *1-59462-001-6* **$30.95**
In no branch of human knowledge has there been a more lively increase of the spirit of research during the past few years than in the study of Psychology, Concentration and Mental Discipline. The requests for authentic lessons in Thought Control, Mental Discipline and...   New Age/Business Pages 422

☐ **The Lesser Key Of Solomon Goetia** by *L. W. de Laurence*   ISBN: *1-59462-092-X* **$9.95**
This translation of the first book of the "Lernegton" which is now for the first time made accessible to students of Talismanic Magic was done, after careful collation and edition, from numerous Ancient Manuscripts in Hebrew, Latin, and French...   New Age/Occult Pages 92

☐ **Rubaiyat Of Omar Khayyam** by *Edward Fitzgerald*   ISBN:*1-59462-332-5* **$13.95**
Edward Fitzgerald, whom the world has already learned, in spite of his own efforts to remain within the shadow of anonymity, to look upon as one of the rarest poets of the century, was born at Bredfield, in Suffolk, on the 31st of March, 1809. He was the third son of John Purcell...   Music Pages 172

☐ **Ancient Law** by *Henry Maine*   ISBN: *1-59462-128-4* **$29.95**
The chief object of the following pages is to indicate some of the earliest ideas of mankind, as they are reflected in Ancient Law, and to point out the relation of those ideas to modern thought.   Religiom/History Pages 452

☐ **Far-Away Stories** by *William J. Locke*   ISBN: *1-59462-129-2* **$19.45**
"Good wine needs no bush," but a collection of mixed vintages does. And this book is just such a collection. Some of the stories I do not want to remain buried for ever in the museum files of dead magazine-numbers an author's not unpardonable vanity..."   Fiction Pages 272

☐ **Life of David Crockett** by *David Crockett*   ISBN: *1-59462-250-7* **$27.45**
"Colonel David Crockett was one of the most remarkable men of the times in which he lived. Born in humble life, but gifted with a strong will, an indomitable courage, and unremitting perseverance...   Biographies/New Age Pages 424

☐ **Lip-Reading** by *Edward Nitchie*   ISBN: *1-59462-206-X* **$25.95**
Edward B. Nitchie, founder of the New York School for the Hard of Hearing, now the Nitchie School of Lip-Reading, Inc, wrote "LIP-READING Principles and Practice". The development and perfecting of this meritorious work on lip-reading was an undertaking...   How-to Pages 400

☐ **A Handbook of Suggestive Therapeutics, Applied Hypnotism, Psychic Science**   ISBN: *1-59462-214-0* **$24.95**
by *Henry Munro*
     Health/New Age/Health/Self-help Pages 376

☐ **A Doll's House: and Two Other Plays** by *Henrik Ibsen*   ISBN: *1-59462-112-8* **$19.95**
Henrik Ibsen created this classic when in revolutionary 1848 Rome. Introducing some striking concepts in playwriting for the realist genre, this play has been studied the world over.   Fiction/Classics/Plays 308

☐ **The Light of Asia** by *sir Edwin Arnold*   ISBN: *1-59462-204-3* **$13.95**
In this poetic masterpiece, Edwin Arnold describes the life and teachings of Buddha. The man who was to become known as Buddha to the world was born as Prince Gautama of India but he rejected the worldly riches and abandoned the reigns of power when...   Religion/History/Biographies Pages 170

☐ **The Complete Works of Guy de Maupassant** by *Guy de Maupassant*   ISBN: *1-59462-157-8* **$16.95**
"For days and days, nights and nights, I had dreamed of that first kiss which was to consecrate our engagement, and I knew not on what spot I should put my lips..."   Fiction/Classics Pages 240

☐ **The Art of Cross-Examination** by *Francis L. Wellman*   ISBN: *1-59462-309-0* **$26.95**
Written by a renowned trial lawyer, Wellman imparts his experience and uses case studies to explain how to use psychology to extract desired information through questioning.   How-to/Science/Reference Pages 408

☐ **Answered or Unanswered?** by *Louisa Vaughan*   ISBN: *1-59462-248-5* **$10.95**
Miracles of Faith in China
     Religion Pages 112

☐ **The Edinburgh Lectures on Mental Science (1909)** by *Thomas*   ISBN: *1-59462-008-3* **$11.95**
This book contains the substance of a course of lectures recently given by the writer in the Queen Street Hail, Edinburgh. Its purpose is to indicate the Natural Principles governing the relation between Mental Action and Material Conditions...   New Age/Psychology Pages 148

☐ **Ayesha** by *H. Rider Haggard*   ISBN: *1-59462-301-5* **$24.95**
Verily and indeed it is the unexpected that happens! Probably if there was one person upon the earth from whom the Editor of this, and of a certain previous history, did not expect to hear again...   Classics Pages 380

☐ **Ayala's Angel** by *Anthony Trollope*   ISBN: *1-59462-352-X* **$29.95**
The two girls were both pretty, but Lucy who was twenty-one who supposed to be simple and comparatively unattractive, whereas Ayala was credited, as her Bombwhat romantic name might show, with poetic charm and a taste for romance. Ayala when her father died was nineteen...   Fiction Pages 484

☐ **The American Commonwealth** by *James Bryce*   ISBN: *1-59462-286-8* **$34.45**
An interpretation of American democratic political theory. It examines political mechanics and society from the perspective of Scotsman James Bryce
     Politics Pages 572

☐ **Stories of the Pilgrims** by *Margaret P. Pumphrey*   ISBN: *1-59462-116-0* **$17.95**
This book explores pilgrims religious oppression in England as well as their escape to Holland and eventual crossing to America on the Mayflower, and their early days in New England...   History Pages 268

QTY

The Fasting Cure *by Sinclair Upton* ISBN: *1-59462-222-1* **$13.95**

In the Cosmopolitan Magazine for May, 1910, and in the Contemporary Review (London) for April, 1910, I published an article dealing with my experiences in fasting. I have written a great many magazine articles, but never one which attracted so much attention... New Age/Self Help/Health Pages 164

☐

Hebrew Astrology *by Sepharial* ISBN: *1-59462-308-2* **$13.45**

In these days of advanced thinking it is a matter of common observation that we have left many of the old landmarks behind and that we are now pressing forward to greater heights and to a wider horizon than that which represented the mind-content of our progenitors... Astrology Pages 144

☐

Thought Vibration or The Law of Attraction in the Thought World ISBN: *1-59462-127-6* **$12.95**

by William Walker Atkinson *Psychology/Religion Pages 144*

☐

Optimism *by Helen Keller* ISBN: *1-59462-108-X* **$15.95**

Helen Keller was blind, deaf, and mute since 19 months old, yet famously learned how to overcome these handicaps, communicate with the world, and spread her lectures promoting optimism. An inspiring read for everyone... Biographies/Inspirational Pages 84

☐

Sara Crewe *by Frances Burnett* ISBN: *1-59462-360-0* **$9.45**

In the first place, Miss Minchin lived in London. Her home was a large, dull, tall one, in a large, dull square, where all the houses were alike, and all the sparrows were alike, and where all the door-knockers made the same heavy sound... Childrens/Classic Pages 88

☐

The Autobiography of Benjamin Franklin *by Benjamin Franklin* ISBN: *1-59462-135-7* **$24.95**

The Autobiography of Benjamin Franklin has probably been more extensively read than any other American historical work, and no other book of its kind has had such ups and downs of fortune. Franklin lived for many years in England, where he was agent... Biographies/History Pages 332

☐

Name	
Email	
Telephone	
Address	
City, State ZIP	

☐ **Credit Card**   ☐ **Check / Money Order**

Credit Card Number	
Expiration Date	
Signature	

Please Mail to: Book Jungle
PO Box 2226
Champaign, IL 61825
or Fax to: 630-214-0564

ORDERING INFORMATION

web: *www.bookjungle.com*
email: *sales@bookjungle.com*
fax: *630-214-0564*
mail: *Book Jungle PO Box 2226 Champaign, IL 61825*
or PayPal *to sales@bookjungle.com*

Please contact us for bulk discounts

DIRECT-ORDER TERMS

**20% Discount if You Order
Two or More Books**
Free Domestic Shipping!
Accepted: Master Card, Visa,
Discover, American Express

www.ingramcontent.com/pod-product-compliance
Lightning Source LLC
LaVergne TN
LVHW061225060426
835509LV00012B/1435